About the Author

I love being a mother and a wife and going on long country walks with our two dogs. I love to relax by reading. I have always loved getting lost in a book and going into that author's world of words. It provided me a way to escape the real world whilst growing up.

Hidden Torture
A Face Behind a Masquerade Mask

Lily Di Giovanni

Hidden Torture
A Face Behind a Masquerade Mask

Olympia Publishers
London

www.olympiapublishers.com
OLYMPIA PAPERBACK EDITION

Copyright © Lily Di Giovanni 2020

A CIP catalogue record for this title is
available from the British Library.

ISBN: 978-1-78830-826-7

This is a work of creative nonfiction. The events are portrayed to the
best of the author's memory. While all the stories in this book are
true, some names and identifying details have been changed to
protect the privacy of the people involved.

First Published in 2020

Olympia Publishers
Tallis House
2 Tallis Street
London
EC4Y 0AB

Printed in Great Britain

Dedication

To all men, women and children who have suffered abuse;
we are not victims but strong survivors.

Acknowledgements

Thank you to my publishers for helping me put together my book and getting my words out there. Thanks for taking a chance on me. I would also like to say thank you to Kristina for the help and the support, whenever I needed it, in the process of bringing this book together – many thanks.

I want to thank my husband and children for all the support, comfort and understanding. You helped me more then you could ever know.

To those close friends that were there for me and by my side every step of the way, I will always be forever grateful.

I have had new relationships form in the last few years that I cherish and will have for ever.

To one very special lady, she knows who she is. Who I will always be eternally grateful to. Who is warm, kind and generous, who has opened her heart and family, to love another child. I say Sincerely THANK YOU, for everything that you and all that your family have done.

Chapter 1

How do you start something that is so difficult to put into words, especially when you have never done anything like this before?

When you go to a friend because you need to talk to them, they will always say, "Keep calm, I'll make a brew and let's start from the beginning." So here goes...

Let's start from the beginning or from when my memory first starts to remember anything...

My earliest memory is around the age of four, maybe five. I cannot recall what had happened, but my memory starts from me being in the hospital as a patient on the children's ward. I remember being in hospital a while, and I can rarely remember my parents ever visiting me. What is so clear as though it happened yesterday is having scans or x-rays done on me. I remember bright lights of the scan room and being wheeled there on a bed from the ward to the x-rays. I can recall two separate occasions; on one visit to the x-ray my mother was walking beside my bed along the corridor. On the second occasion that I can remember it was my father walking beside my bed whilst being escorted to the x-ray room. I remember being taken to x-ray two or three different times, the big shining lights blinding my eyes as if I was looking into the sun whilst doing as I was told by the staff members so they could take some form of pictures of my head. I always lay down on my hospital bed being pushed to x-ray, then I was taken back to the children's ward. How long I was in hospital for seemed like weeks at the time. If I had to answer that question now, I would say I was in for a week, maybe two.

I remember a lady coming to pick me up from the hospital; she was from the Children's Services. I can recall she had a small white car. She put me in the front seat next to her and put my seat belt on and gave me a bag of sweets. She never took me back to my parents or my family home. I can remember pulling up outside this lovely big house; there was a man and woman waiting on the doorstep for us. They knew who I was, and I remember them both giving me a hug. The lady from the Children's Services then explained to me that I was going to be staying here for a while.

The period that I stayed there, the woman from Children's Services would often come to pick me up and we would meet up with my parents in the town center of where I was from, so they could spend some time with me. Then later on that day I would be returned back to the foster family where I was staying.

I don't know how long I was with that foster family for, but Children's Services after a period of time returned me back to the care of my parents.

I remember the day I had to leave the foster family. I really didn't want to go back home. I wanted to stay with my foster family. That was one of the happiest times of my childhood being with them. I still have memories of being chased around the house, being caught and tickled; I was always laughing and so very happy. The beautiful wooden staircase that went round in a curve. The smells from baking in the kitchen, smells of the bushes in the garden especially after it rained where the smells of the bushes and flowers were heightened. I sometimes got transported back to that time when I used to walk home from school in the rain, walking past a certain bush and I would get a whiff of that same scent; it would always put a smile on my face. They had an older daughter around high school age. I would wave goodbye to her on the doorstep with my foster mother and she would wave back in return whilst going to school. On a couple of occasions, I remember her having her ballet pumps or tap shoes over her shoulder. The big party that they threw for me the day before I left them. Those memories I have always cherished and kept them close to my heart. I will always remember how special both my foster mother and father were to me; they gave me an insight of what it was like to be part of a normal life, to be a happy little girl who felt loved.

People's names have been changed to protect their true identity. The true facts and events of what really happened…

I was only four years of age at the time of this event. Mr Cooper from the NSPCC visited my home after receiving information to the effect that I had been seen at the back-bedroom window with facial bruising that was evident from such a distance. Mr Cooper had paid a visit mid-afternoon, but there was no reply. He returned later the same day at teatime and was received by my mother. Her initial response was to turn around and called upstairs to my father, "It's the NSPCC." Mr Cooper stated he had called to see me as a report had been received that I had severe bruises to my face. My mother promptly said that he was wasting his time, that I was away at my grandmother's. Mr Cooper said that he had reason to believe that this was not true and suggested that my father should be involved in this discussion, but he also denied that I was at home for twenty minutes. Mr Cooper stated that he was left with no alternative but to call the police to intervene in terms of search and removal. Eventually, I was brought downstairs and the bruising was very evident: circular bruising round the left eye, black and blue, deep red coloring and older yellow bruising around the right eye and forehead.

The interview was very difficult from the onset, mainly because of what Mr Cooper felt of my father's personality disorders. My dad very quickly began to come across very volatile, but otherwise of average intelligence. Mr Cooper found it difficult to talk to me. He asked me how I had come to have the bruises on my face. My mother's answer was that I fell in the bedroom on the cot. My father's answer was that I had fallen downstairs and banged myself against a cupboard. My father commented that Mr Cooper would think he had been battering the child. He did admit, however, that he did hit me if I was naughty, but only slapped me on the bottom. Mr Cooper stated he began to talk in general terms of the needs of the child to be seen in hospital, and although he stated this on two occasions he was refused and had to talk in terms of seeking police assistance to achieve this. At this point my father said he would agree to me going to hospital, but my dad would take me in his car. This was done, and Mr Cooper followed us in his car.

Two hours later were spent in the Accident Medical Department and I was seen by a doctor who was the Senior Casualty Officer. I had my skull x-rayed later. I chatted a little about hurting myself on a cot, but as I was talking to the doctor who was looking after me, he felt there was need for further investigations of myself in terms of skeletal survey. He also felt the need for the opinion of the Consultant Pediatrician and, therefore, recommended that I should be admitted. The doctor was also very suspicious because my father was telling the same story about me having fallen in the bedroom. The reason the interview took so long was because my father was extremely volatile, and very threatening on occasions: one minute he was agreeable to voluntary action to take me into care and minutes later he was not, varying from being calm and pleasant to being quite violent.

Mr Cooper talked to him about taking police action in seeking a POS. Eventually, my father calmed down, but he was constantly making conditions and it was quite obvious that he was seeking to keep control of the situation. He agreed that I could stay in hospital on condition that I stayed only until 10:00 am the following morning. If investigations were not finished by then, he would be taking me home. That evening after I was admitted Mr Cooper went back to see my mother at approximately 21:15. My father had been in touch by telephone when I had been admitted. Mr Cooper did feel that she may earlier have been frightened to say what had really happened and, therefore, went back to give her another opportunity to explain the bruising. She was much too calm under the circumstances, showing little or no emotion, and she didn't get upset.

Later that evening Mr Cooper telephoned the local police station and spoke to Sergeant Brown and acquainted him of what had been happening. It was decided that he should meet him at the police station and put him in the picture. DC Walker was in the office and had become aware of the enquiries and remembered the family from a previous visit he had made. He spoke with Mr Cooper that evening. He also described my father as obsessive, irritable and unpredictable and referred to his visit to this home approximately two years earlier to investigate some incident. In the course of speaking to my dad and mum he heard a noise and thought it was a dog in a cupboard, but in fact it was me locked up in the upstairs bedroom, and I appeared quite miserable. My father indicated that that was the way of dealing with the child when she misbehaved – they would lock me in the bedroom.

The following day Mr Cooper and the NSPCC had liaised with police, mainly focusing on a joint investigation with DC Walker, who had been instructed by the Detective Chief Inspector that this was to be treated as a case of child abuse. Mr Cooper also contacted the Child Abuse Register, and spoke to Dr Adams, who was expressing the opinion that he was unhappy about the situation and with the explanations given. If my parents would not co-operate in terms of an admission to hospital a POS should be considered. When Mr Cooper checked with the sister on the ward at 13:30 on Monday, she was advised that my father had telephoned several times, very anxious and threatening to remove me.

By the middle of that afternoon, assisted by Inspector Barns, a POS order was made for eight days. On Tuesday 6th May 1986 Mr Cooper conferred with a colleague, Mark Bridges of the local office, who recalled his feelings when he visited the home. His feelings confirmed Mr Cooper's about my father being a very dangerous and unstable man, and it was on the basis of this that it was decided to have an urgent case conference. Also, on Tuesday, at about 13:00 my father telephoned Mr Cooper at his office to ask what was happening. He was advised that a case conference was to take place, and he was told that Mr Cooper would visit him afterwards. My father wanted to know about all facts and about further steps. Mr Cooper stated that he felt fairly safe in saying to him that one of the case conference decisions may indeed be to seek the authority of a juvenile court, or bring the matter before the juvenile court, before I could be returned home. To Mr Cooper's surprise this did not get a word of response, but my father went on to talk about what the conference could do, if they were not abusing me. Mr Cooper rang my parents on the 7th May and left a message on the telephone answering machine advising that Mr Cooper would ring again the following day. On Wednesday morning it was a very long and difficult telephone conversation, mainly because it was quite repetitive on how they functioned as parents and whether it was safe to allow me to return home. Mr Cooper talked in terms of answers to questions which needed clarification. At a later stage in the discussion it was suggested by my father that perhaps it would help if they said that she, meaning my mother, got upset when I was making a fuss and my mother pushed me away so that I fell against the hall heater. So yet again the story changes on how I got all the bruises.

The Outcome...

Mr Dalton explained that it had been decided at the previous conference to meet today to review the situation following the court hearing on Monday 9th June.

Mr Cooper of the NSPCC stated that, at the hearing on 9th June, the case had been dismissed and that he had one or two observations he wished to make about the hearing last Monday. He explained that he was restricted as to the extent he could comment because there was just a possibility that the social will be taking further legal steps to protect me from what he felt was a VERY DANGEROUS SITUATION. The first point, which relates to the dismissal of the application, is that in their opinion there was considerable mismanagement on the part of the court itself, and there were one or two points to put forward to support this: (i) the bench consisted of two male magistrates, which is contrary to normal practice in juvenile courts, and (ii) NSPCC went to court prepared to apply for a further Interim Care Order because Dr Adams, Consultant Pediatrician, was unavailable and they thought that the court would readily agree to a further Interim Order and NSPCC had advised the other witnesses not to attend and, therefore on Monday were not prepared for a full hearing. The application for an Interim Care Order was opposed by the two solicitors representing myself and my parents, and the court accepted this and ruled that the NSPCC should offer as much evidence that was offered at the first hearing when the Interim Care Order was made.

The second point about the court's mismanagement was that the clerk of the court must have known that it was likely to be of some length. At the same time, he must have known that one of the magistrates had a personal appointment that afternoon which meant that he would have to leave the court. At 13:15 they were told of this and that the hearing could not continue. There was strong opposition by all three solicitors but the hearing was adjourned until 17:30 and subsequently, the hearing went on until the magistrate retired at approximately 23:15 on Monday night, when it is contrary to advised practice in juvenile courts to proceed to such a late hour in the day. The magistrates returned with their decision that the application was dismissed and that I should be returned home at the earliest opportunity, this despite the fact that we had been allowed by the opposing solicitors to produce to the courts information about who the other witnesses would be and what they were likely to say.

Mr Cooper felt that the court might have been influenced by the evidence of the Guardian ad Interim, Mr Hardy, whose opinion was that the child, meaning myself, had not been abused and that I should be returned "home immediately". In his evidence, Mr Hardy had stated that he had seen me twice in the foster home. The first visit was brief, approximately ten minutes, and the second visit approximately an hour. During the course of this hour, he asked me on at least six occasions, "How did you hurt your eye?" He also said that the time interval between the question was deliberately varied but that on each of the six occasions, in response to the question I said, "I fell on the cot; Mummy and Daddy didn't smack me." Mr Hardy also visited the home and interviewed my parents twice and was convinced that the child had not been abused.

Mr Cooper wished to record their continuing anxiety about me and also to say that they believed that the court's decisions had PLACED ME IN EVEN GREATER DANGER THAN I WAS IN BEFORE. IF WE ARE RIGHT IN OUR BELIEFS THAT SHE HAS BEEN ABUSED, THEN THE PARENTS HAVE NOW SUCCEEDED IN "GETTING AWAY WITH IT". It could, therefore, be thought that they might now be feeling an increased sense of security and might believe that any further abuse is likely to be identified or dealt with adequately. The child has not got the full protection of the law in this situation and, therefore, some form of continuation by the society is being considered. The society is unable to lodge an appeal, but there is another legal process that can be applied and may be applied in this case by NSPCC.

Mr Dalton explained that whilst I was on an Interim Care Order, access had been allowed to the parents on three days a week, Monday, Wednesday and Friday afternoons from 14:00 to 15:30. Ms Nichol said that this went off very well. Mother had attended on every occasion and father had been there on most occasions. Grandmother had been three times. My father's attitude to Ms Nichol was good and although at first, he had said no to voluntary supervision, when Ms Nichol had taken me back after the court hearing, he had said that she was welcome to call any time she liked.

Ms Nichol mentioned that on Monday, my foster mother had reported that I had come out in an eczema-type rash and that, also in the last week, I had been soiling my pants. My foster mother thought that I had probably been fretting.

Mr Dalton agreed with Mr Cooper that it may be a little difficult ensuring me protection in the future but that whilst the parents are willing to accept voluntary supervision, it should be offered and felt that my father may be more amenable to a female social worker then a male.

Mrs Jenkins asked if it was known whether Dr Adams would have enlarged on his statement in court, and Mr Cooper said he would have been examined by their solicitor and would have had to offer comments on how it could be that a child had bruises being several days old. He felt the court would have considered this as a major issue and that the court had made its decision on limited evidence. The medical report was not satisfactory at all, as it did not give any explanation as to how I had received these injuries and it was because of this that their application was that there should be a further Interim Care Order. They felt the case could have been adjourned if they had been allowed to do so. When requesting a further period of interim care, they had said they could present the full facts to the court on Thursday – the earliest opportunity after the doctor's return to work. This was opposed by the defense solicitor and the court ruled against the NSPCC.

My own personal thoughts and feelings…

Now I have read the evidence that I have to hand, I have very mixed emotions. I have a volcano of anger that builds up inside of me. I have re-read my child service reports over and over again – a few times whilst writing this book – and in my opinion, I was severely let down by so many people. I went through life always thinking that the children services were the ones that let me down the most, this was up till about five years ago when I was given my children services reports and realized that the courts themselves played a huge and disappointing role. The system is there to protect vulnerable children like me, especially at such a young age as I was. When I went back over the evidence again, to me, the first mistake was allowing my father to take me to the hospital. The reason I say this is because the evidence stated that when my father put me in the car, we were on the driveway for approximately ten minutes; it was just the two of us sat in the car. So was he coaxing me on what to say? Was I being threatened by him? If I spoke out and told the truth of how received my injuries… Ten minutes is enough time to put the fear into a small child, plus add on the drive time it would take to get to the hospital that would have been an extra twenty minutes, give or take, depending on traffic. So my father had a good half an hour where it was just me and him alone in that car; plenty of time for him to manipulate a young child's mind. In my opinion, Mr

Cooper from the NSPCC should have been more forceful and adamant and taken me in his car with one of my parents, especially if his concerns were heightened after the reports and once seeing me and the bruises.

Secondly, why weren't my parents' change of stories ever taken into consideration? Till this day and even in the evidence of the reports I have to hand, the bruising I had received was never explained. First, it was 'I fell from a cot,' then that changed to 'she fell down the stairs,' and thirdly my father said, "Maybe we should say it was her mother pushing her away and by doing that, she ended up hitting her head on the heater." Now I'm no detective, but even I would be questioning which one was it. Deep down, I feel they had physically abused me and they were doing what they did best: trying to do whatever they could to protect their backs. However, you cannot hide from the fact that I had multiple bruises; some had faded, some were still there but were a few days old and some were very recent ones, as was described in a variety of colours. I also wonder if the hospital had taken any photographs of my face and the markings when I was admitted and if so, would these have been used at a later date if they were needed?

Thirdly, I have concerns in regard to Mr Hardy the Guardian ad Interim, even though he only saw me twice and apparently repeatedly questioned me, "How did you hurt your eye?" Was he not concerned or slightly worried with my blunt response for a little girl? Especially as my response never changed; it was always the same, "I fell on the cot," followed up with, "Mummy and Daddy never smacked me." Now, why would a four year old child even say that, when that wasn't even mentioned or part of the question being asked… unless a child has been coaxed to say that? Personally, it would make me sit back and think to myself, why would a child offer a line like that when I never mentioned the parents? Maybe then ask the child why I would think that her mummy and daddy had smacked her. That's just me though, but it is a small piece of common sense.

Lastly, my foster mother also voiced her concerns in regard to me starting to soil myself in the last week of me being with them, thinking that I was probably fretting. To me, does this not display a child in distress or being fearful about something? No doubt I would have been informed by someone that I was to be returned back home and that may have terrified me, because I do definitely remember wanting to stay with my foster family and not return back to my family home. So even writing this little bit myself, there were still a lot of red flags flying around and being displayed in clear view; additionally, I was clearly being ignored. I'm no professional, but common sense should prevail should it not? If I can see the red flags or hear the alarm bells then why weren't they acted on? I did, however, once bring this up to my mother a few years back when I wanted answers – she did open up a little bit, but not much. My mother only talked about that one event and she literally said to me, "It was your dad; he was always giving you a beating of some kind and there were times when there was no reason for them. It simply could have been that he was having a bad day, or things weren't going his way. There was a bigger reason than all them though: it was because you weren't his."

Essentially, the moment he entered our lives, I was his personal human punching bag; I never stood a chance really then did I? In my own personal opinion, my mother – even though she had suffered herself – was just as guilty if not worse, if truth be told, because she knew it was going on and she allowed it to happen time and time again. It was like a continuous cycle being repeated with no ending in sight.

Chapter 2

Once I returned to the care of my parents…

I cannot recall the time scale of when things started going wrong from when I was returned to my family home. I know that it was straight away, maybe a few months later.

This is my account and memories of what I can clearly remember, of being mistreated by my parents. I was in the back bedroom of our house and I slept on the floor on a couple of sheets and a blanket to cover me up. The floor didn't have carpet down; it was just the normal floorboards that houses have. I can remember clothes always being thrown into the middle of my floor and piling up. One night I woke up through the early hours of the night needing the toilet, and because I went to the toilet and flushed the chain, I woke up my parents and this actually angered my father, as I remember he had to be up really early for work. I was shouted at and was smacked hard with a slipper or shoe right on my bottom. After this had happened, it made me scared to go to the toilet through the night again, because I didn't want to be punished. So the next time when I did wake up through the night needing to go to the bathroom, instead of going to the toilet, I would go and wee on the pile of clothes that were in the middle of my bedroom floor. I did this on a couple of occasions before I was caught out by my mother, probably because of the smell coming from the clothes. My mother must have told my father because when I got home from school, I recall her saying, "Your dad wants you upstairs." I remember going upstairs and he was waiting for me on the landing of our house and I remember him asking me, "Have you been weeing on your bedroom floor?" I don't know if I admitted to it or not; to be honest, I probably may have lied and said I hadn't. I will never ever forget the punishment that I received that day. It has stayed with me ever since. Mother had come upstairs as well, so there the three of us were, myself, mother and father. My mother knelt in front of me and started to undress me. Once I was completely undressed and naked, my father went behind me and grabbed my arms and tied some kind of rope or string around my wrists behind my back, so I couldn't move my arms. Mother had rolled up a pair of socks into a ball and held my nose so that I opened my mouth. She stuffed that rolled up the pair of socks into my mouth. Once that was done my mouth was then taped over so that the rolled-up socks wouldn't fall out, I guess, to stop me from shouting or screaming out. Then both my parents would carry me into the bathroom and put me in the bath with my head directly under the taps. Next thing I knew the cold tap was put on full blast with my head being held underneath it. I remember kicking my legs and trying to scream; all the time there they were, my parents holding me down, trying to keep me still. My account of this event is so very clear in my head. It could be as though it only happened yesterday, the pain of that cold water rushing down on you, the pain of it going into my eyes and going up my nose, hardly able to breathe. Thinking back to the pain of it now I would say it felt like a thousand knives hitting you all at once.

This punishment did not happen just the once, but on a few occasions, and it was not just for needing the loo through the night; this style of treatment was used for other things too.

Another time this happened was again needing the toilet through the night, so I climbed into the cot that was in my room and weed on the blankets that were piled up in there. Again, it was my mother that noticed what I had done. She told my father, and again I got punished in the exact way as mentioned earlier, stripped down naked, my arms tied behind my back, rolled-up pair of socks in my mouth which was followed by being taped over, carried into the bathtub, head held under the taps and cold tap was put on full blast. Again, it was mother that undressed me and put the socks in my mouth and my father that tied my arms behind my back and taped over my mouth.

The third time I actually would wee on these big teddies that I had. They were so big; there was a huge dog teddy that was half the width of my bedroom and a super large brown bear. I did wee on both of these; how many times, though, I cannot recall. I do remember blaming it on my sibling when I got asked if it was me that had done it. I can't remember which parent had found out about it, but anyway I got the same punishment, but this time slightly different. It was my father that undressed me and stuffed the rolled-up socks into my mouth, and it was my mother that tied my arms behind my back and put tape over my mouth. I was carried into the bathroom and laid in the bath again; my head was under the taps, but this time the plug was put into the plug hole and when the cold tap was put on full blast, not only was the water stinging my eyes and going up my nose, but the bath was filling up also. My mother was holding down my legs to stop me from moving. My father was holding my head under the water as the bath filled up. He would then lift my head up out of the water and shout words at me that I cannot recall. After shouting at me he would dunk my head back under the water and hold it there. He would repeat this, bring my head back up so I could breathe but he would shout and then dunk my head back under the water and hold me there. I just couldn't move, I couldn't wiggle, even though I tried. My whole body was being held still under the water by my parents. I was only six years old when this extreme punishment was put upon me.

Thinking about it now, why in hell would you think of punishing your child in such a way? Where do these thoughts come from?

Going a little bit forward, I was stealing food at school. I would make an excuse to the teachers, saying, "I needed the toilet"; instead I would go into the corridor and into the other kids' lunch boxes and steal their food, because I was so hungry, and eat it in the toilets. At home I had to get myself up and dressed and because my mother never got up to make me breakfast, I had to climb onto the kitchen work top and eat pure sugar from the bag and make sure I didn't get caught. School had caught me out for stealing and got my mother into school to inform her of what I had been doing. When she got me home, I was sent to my room until my father returned home. Obviously, my mother would have told him all about what the school had informed her of my stealing from the other boys' and girls' lunch boxes. My father got me over his knee, pulled down both my pants and underwear and got my mother to use her belt, the buckle part, and she belted me with that bloody belt five times, and if she didn't do it hard enough, then he would tell her to do it again. I'm sure he did it on purpose, wanting her to continue belting me many times; I feel he was actually getting off on it, thinking about it now. There he was, me bent over his knee with my little bare bottom being hit many times by my mother whilst he watched my bum getting redder and redder, being severely marked each time that buckle hit my skin. What was he getting from it? Also, as I look back, my mother would have known what would have happened, she knew I would be punished in some way, so why didn't she keep it to herself and protect her child? But no, what was she wanting from him or what did she want to show him? That she was loyal and wouldn't keep anything from him. That he could trust her to be truthful at all times. I just don't get it, any of it.

This was, sorry to say, the start of my stealing days. I stole from school, from the local supermarket and local shops, even stole from within the home, all because I was always hungry.

There was a time that I stole two kit kats from the fridge. When I was asked if I had taken them by my father, I lied and said no; I think I actually said that my mother must have eaten them. I do recall my father saying that if I told the truth that nothing would happen to me and that he would be proud of the fact that I admitted to stealing. When I did admit to taking the chocolate bars, my father dragged me into the bathroom and put my head down the toilet and flushed the chain. As he put my head down the toilet, he actually bashed my head on the side of the toilet, and I was bleeding from a cut above my left eye. I actually have the scar on my left eyebrow to show for it. So that shows my father's word meant jack. If I lied, I got punished, and even when I told the truth, I still got punished. Talk about confusing a little girl, no matter what she does she cannot win either way.

My mother was quick to get in on my stealing, especially from the local supermarket. I remember this long blue puffa winter coat that I had. It had an inside pocket and there was a hole inside the lining; it was ideal when it came to stealing. My mother would send me to the shop and tell me what she wanted. She would give me money for some of the items; the rest I would have to shoplift. She was so pleased with me when I got home and surprisingly, she never once told my father what I was doing; this she kept a secret between the two of us. That was until I got caught shoplifting by the security; I was taken home and my mother wasn't happy at all. When she told my father, he for the first time wasn't angry or mad. I never got punished, but instead he had a smile on his face and had a laugh and joke about it and his words to me were something along the lines of "all well, we've all done it at least once, the trick is not to get caught. Don't be so stupid next time", and that was it.

There were a few occasions when Mother would take us on the bus to go and do the weekly shop in the next town. She would always take with her quite a few bags. As we were going around the shop, I would notice that she would put items in the bags bit by bit, and some of the food into the trolley. By the time we had got around the shop and she had got everything we needed, as she would approach the checkouts she would give me the bags that she had filled up and tell me to go outside with them and wait for her to pay for the little shopping that was actually in the trolley. I remember thinking at the time: she's going to get caught doing this. Every time she came out with the shopping, she actually purchased I was always shocked. How the hell did she get away with it? I don't know. Now, though, as I look back, she used me as a buffer; it was me that would get stopped with three or four bags of shopping that was being stolen. My mother never had the stolen goods in her hands, she was using me. What can I say? She taught me from a young age to be good at shoplifting for the future.

The scariest time that I stole something I was around the age of eleven, I think. It wasn't chocolate or a bag of sweets or something that my mother sent me to the shops for; well, I guess in a way it was. This one occasion she actually came with me because I needed a new pair of shoes. This particular superstore had all these shoes out on display in different sizes, so you never needed to ask anyone if they had a certain style in a shoe size that fits. Anyway, there was a lovely pair of shoes that I really did like, and mother dearest said try them on, which obviously I did, and the shop had two or three pairs left in my size. As we were walking back home, mother said wear the worst pair of shoes I had and walk back to the shop and try the shoes on again. This time, though, when I try on the new shoes, leave my old shoes in the box and just walk out of the supermarket via the back entrance wearing those new shoes. Boy, my heart was racing so much that day, I was always looking over my shoulder double-checking that no-one was around the aisle or no-one was watching me. I swapped those shoes over so quick and walked past the checkouts straight out the back entrance and just ran for it. It was lucky that I was a pretty good runner at the time.

I could go on and on about this particular event in my life, as there were many occasions where I had to steal, whether it was for my mother or later on when it was for myself, especially stealing makeup and selling it at school. But I don't want to, because I closed that door to the past so many years ago. Also, it makes me feel so ashamed of myself. I stopped stealing full stop at fifteen.

I do remember roughly in this time scale Children's Services came and made a few visits to the house. It was a gentleman that came on both occasions. From my memory I would say that he was probably around middle age, greying hair with a beard and moustache. My parents must have known he was coming to pay a visit to the house and speak to me. The reason I say this is because they both talked to me beforehand, they told me where to sit, so that they could watch me through the glass above the kitchen door from the stairs. They got a tape recorder and placed it just behind the microwave in the kitchen. So when I was asked questions I couldn't answer honestly, as the conversation was being recorded. After the gentleman left the house my parents would take the tape recorder upstairs and listen to it.

I was moved from the large back bedroom into the front smaller bedroom of our house. There was a big cheese plant near my bed in the corner of the room. I started waking up again through the night for the toilet. I would use the cheese plant to wee in so the mud would absorb the pee. The reason I did this was because going to the toilet meant that I would have to walk past my parents' bedroom, and my bedroom door creaked and there was a loose floorboard that was noisy. So the fear of waking up my father took hold of me. Anyway, after a while the leaves of the cheese plant were dying. To this day I don't know how they found out that I was using it as a toilet. I remember getting sent to my bedroom and I could hear my parents from the living room discussing my punishment and I heard my father say, "We could put her head under the tap again." I was so scared of that happening, that I climbed out of my bedroom window onto the covering over the front door and ran away into nearby woods. I stayed hidden there for what seemed like hours. My mother later found me and took me home. Where I was given one hell of a beating, my window got locked and I wasn't allowed out of the house.

Another hazy memory I have was when the back bedroom was being decorated. I think I was in trouble at school. I must have done something wrong as I remember I was facing the wall in the back bedroom and my father was using some form of small heated spotlight. I recall as he was getting closer and closer to me, he would move the light with him. Now as soon as he was right next to me, he put the spotlight directly onto my lower leg, and boy, can I still remember the burning of it. I remember wearing my school socks up to my knee so it covered the burn, but when I got home and my mother took my socks off they were stuck to my skin and it hurt so much because my socks would take some of the skin away and it would bleed and be weepy for ages.

Evidence of reports…

Ms Nichol had visited the home in December 1986 and February 1987. In April 1987 Ms Nichol had received a message from Mrs Seaton saying that she had an anonymous report of shouting and the sound of furniture being moved in the household the previous night. The noise started at approximately 23:00. My father had been heard shouting, "You've wet the bed, haven't you?" and I was heard to reply in a frightened voice that I had not. The report also suggested that a thud was heard against the wall and a scream.

After a discussion with my school headmaster and Mrs Seaton, it was decided that Ms Nichol would visit and confront the parents with this report. My father actually admitted that it was partly true. He had shouted at me for wetting the bed but had not smacked me. He said that my mother did most of the shouting, because she had just changed all the beds that same day. I was at school when Ms Nichol had first arrived and my father asked if she would wait until I came back from school. There were marks on my arm but barely visible. My father asked if Ms Nichol wished to strip me down to look for any bruises, but Ms Nichol declined this offer and did not feel it was necessary.

Mrs Seaton was not happy with the attitude of both my parents and said the neighbors worried her as all of them had something to say. The family don't get on with their neighbors and do not have anything to do with them. My father stated that they are very nosy and jealous of what they have got. The house is always immaculate and very well looked after. My father appears a bit of a bully, but although my mother is a very quiet person, she has been seen to hit me and lose her temper with me. In response to this my mother says that she was a battered child herself and this is why she would not do it to her own child.

Ms Nichol felt that the court appearance and the follow-up had really had an effect on them and they are "CONSTANTLY BEING REMINDED ABOUT IT". My father has not been difficult with her and they have a good relationship, but he questions why they should continue to be subjected to all this.

Ms Nichol stated that since the last review the family have been very quiet and there have been no further reports. Ms Nichol had called at my school where my teacher mentioned that on occasions, I was taking other children's lunches. On one occasion I had lunch of my own (fruit) but took a chocolate bar from someone else's lunch box. My headmaster stated that he had only known me since Christmas. There had been problems of light-fingeredness.

Mr Smith reports that whilst on enquiries into another

34

incident involving me, concern was expressed by the residents of a few households in the area which was visited into the physical welfare of the child. There was also an unconfirmed allegation that my mother was acting like a modern day "FAGIN" by sending me out to the nearby supermarket to commit possible offences.

Another report was given to the Children's Services department in 1991 saying that I was having my head held under the tap water and sometimes left in cold water. My mother also allegedly encourages me to go and steal. I have recently been caught stealing but because of my age the store did not inform the police. Last summer I again allegedly ran away from home because I was fed up with getting hit.

In 1988 it was reported by one of the neighbors who had gone into the department of the Children's Services to inform them that I had a bad burn on my lower leg the previous week. Apparently, I had told someone what had happened to my leg, and that I was to keep it a secret. As I was told not to divulge this information by my parents.

The burn to my leg was also reported to Children's Services by my schoolteacher. They were worried as I'd had it for a while and it wasn't getting any better; they were worried I had an infection.

My own personal thoughts and feelings…

Even after writing this chapter, there is some regard to red flags. The evidence states that loud noises were heard one evening and my father was shouting at me, after which you could hear me letting out a scream. This was yet again reported to the authorities and once more nothing was done. You would have thought that the social services would have looked at the history regarding the family, or the times that they had been called out to the property. There were also reports made by my school teachers that I had makings on my upper arms of faded bruises that were becoming barely visible.

When Ms Nichol was given the option by my father to undress me so she could see for herself if there were any other questioning bruises that could possibly hidden, why would he decline that offer? Why didn't she take him up on it and think to herself that he was bluffing? By putting that offer out there, did she think that they had nothing to hide? Once again, they were outsmarted by my parents.

In the report, Mrs Seaton herself states and she was 'not happy with either one of her parents' attitude', and goes even further by saying our neighbours worried her as 'each of them had something to say'. Why was it not a matter of concern when my school teachers informed the social services that, at times, I was actually stealing the other children's lunches?

It even states in my medical reports that I was an extremely skinny child and underweight, because I was starved. Why wasn't this being monitored? I actually had the strength to tell someone about the kind of punishment I was getting at home in regard to being held under the tap. In 1991, I was nine when a neighbour reported this, so that is three years I suffered that kind of hidden torture before I had the guts to speak to someone I trusted.

Once again, though, these reports got swept under the carpet and my parents yet again got away with it. So many different reports, some of them had been called in; at another time, a neighbour actually went into the department to make the report face to face. I had my own guardian angels trying their best to look out for me and do what they could to protect me; unfortunately, to no avail. Why was this allowed to happen? Five to six years after being returned home I suffered and not one person from the children services ever thought how strange it was that they were always being called out to the same address time and time again.

The warning signs were all there, flashing in their damn faces, and my parents once again were allowed to outsmart them. Another thing that always seemed to puzzle me was the time when a gentleman came round to the house to question me on my own, where both my parents were going to be there. Okay, maybe they weren't in the same room as me, but they were still close enough to hear the conversation. Why wasn't I taken to some kind of family centre of some sort and then taken into one of those child friendly rooms, where I could possibly feel safe to open up knowing my parents weren't nearby. Wouldn't that have been the more sensible approach?

My father was known to be a bully, with a controlling personality, who liked to control all things within the household; shouldn't this have been taken into consideration? If this was to happen again in today's day and age, would the same thing be allowed to happen again? I would like to say no, but honestly I don't know. I would like to think that times had changed and now the correct procedures have been put into place and the mistakes of the past had been learnt from; however, you still hear of vulnerable children being let down and falling in-between the cracks, because parents can put on such a good persona. It's like they adopt this mask and by doing this, and being allowed to do it, they are managing to outsmart the authorities. This raises questions about the child services: are they so overwhelmingly under-staffed, or are their caseloads so heavy, that there simply isn't enough manpower to put in enough hours for the job to be done properly and assess each child? If this is the case then the problem is only going to get a lot worse and that in itself is extremely worrying. I fear for those children, like myself, who will suffer; some will probably suffer even more than I did. That isn't a pleasant thought.

Chapter 3

I could now talk about the treatment my mother had to endure before I go forward into the next experience of my life. I think it would be a good idea, actually, to write about what my mother suffered at the hands of my father, as you will get a better picture of later events and decisions that were made, when I get to writing that part.

The earliest memory that I can clearly recall was my mother being kicked and punched of my father whilst she was curled up on the living room floor. I was only about age five or six. I remember that she had to go into hospital. I have witnessed him holding a gun to my mother's head whilst he accused her of having an affair with some guy that lived in our local area, when in fact she wasn't.

I always remember that through the week there wasn't much in the way of arguments; there may have been a few heated debates. However, when Fridays came around you could always count on there being massive bust ups, and huge arguments. Father would always beat up my mother, and the house would get smashed up pretty badly. My father would always make it out that my mother would start it on purpose, making it out that she would wait on purpose for Friday to come around to annoy him because she knew it would spoil his weekends off. Looking back at it now, I'm sure that he looked for reasons to kick off, whether it was because she may not have had his tea ready for him, or that she drank too much at the pub with my grandmother, or that she hadn't done all the housework that was supposed to be done before he got home from work. He just couldn't ever let it go like any normal person, and just look forward to spending his weekend off and enjoy it with his family. Oh no, he could never do that, could he? His way of dealing with it was being a bastard all the time, a bloody psycho nutter.

There was one weekend; it was a Friday, and my mother and grandma had met up at the local pub. We would walk from school to meet them there; it was only about five minutes away, if that. My mother had a little bit too much to drink and she was in a happy mood singing along with my grandma whilst we walked home. I was staying at my grandparents' that night; my mother walked home on her own. A couple of hours later, Grandma got a phone call and left straight away after whispering something to my granddad. About 30 minutes later, my grandparents' house phone started ringing. My granddad answered the call. After a few seconds he came into the living room and told me the phone was for me. It was my grandma on the phone asking me to come home as she needed my help, but not to worry as I will be coming back to hers a little later with her. As I was walking home, I had a feeling that something wasn't right. When I got to the front door my grandmother opened the door and told me not to worry. As I walked into the house my father was in the living room looking as if he was trying to calm himself; you could tell he was angry just by looking at him. As I was heading to the kitchen my grandmother told me not to be scared when I entered the kitchen. My mother was there with blood oozing from her head, her blond hair covered and getting matted with the blood. I have seen my mother in many a state after what my father would do to her, but this this was on another level. I will never forget the way she looked on that night. I guess my fear of my father increased even more then as I knew what he was actually capable of. My grandma told me that she was taking my mother upstairs to put her in the bath to clean her up. She asked me to clean up the kitchen. As I was starting to clean the kitchen up, I went to the sink to fill up the bowl with water and bleach, and there in the sink was a knife covered with blood all over it. I put two and two together and I just knew that was the cause of my mother's injury. My father had stabbed my mother in the head, I later learned on my way back to my grandparents. I was told by grandma to keep it quiet from granddad, as all he knew was that my parents had a huge argument. The kitchen had been smashed up; it was just a massive mess. My grandma later came down from putting my mother to bed and helped me finish cleaning the kitchen. As we left the house grandma told me to wait outside the front door, whilst she went into the living room and had some sort of word with my father. Then the two of us walked back to her house. The next day, as though nothing had happened, my father took my mother to the Grand National for the day. When they came to pick us up, they were having a laugh saying that they both won on the horses they betted on and were so upbeat. It was so surreal going from one extreme to another.

I remember as I got older, from the age of eleven I was seen differently in high school. The reason why, I am sure of this, was because as I started high school, we went on holiday within the first month of me starting. My father would always get me to model my new holiday clothes for him, especially my bikinis and sometimes he would get me and my mother to put on our bikinis together. We would both put on our bikinis and go downstairs into the living room, whilst he sat on the sofa looking at us. He would ask us both to turn around so our backs were to him, then wanting us to turn back around so we were facing him, but we had to do it slowly for him. His reason for doing this was to make sure that they fitted properly or, in my case, didn't make me look too young, as I was wearing women's swimsuits. I remember doing this quite a few times over the years. My mother would always make it known that she could fit into a 15-16-year-old's clothes. So yes, every time she would order new clothes from her catalogue, I couldn't just try the clothes on to see for myself if they fit. My father would always want us to try them on so he could see how they fitted me.

At the age of 13 I was around at my friend's house for the day and I lost track of the time. I got home about an hour later than I was supposed to. My father went mental and lost his rag with me. He punched me in the face twice and broke my nose. I never knew that a nose could bleed so much. My father got me on the kitchen floor and sat on top of me, slapping me across my face; then he got up and kicked me in my back. My mother was in the kitchen the whole time and she never once stepped in to protect me or try and pull my father away. Instead she just stood there and watched it all happening in front of her. After my father had finished punishing me and left the kitchen, the only thing my mother said to me was, "You should have been home on time, it's your own fault, you only have yourself to blame." With that said she left the kitchen and went wherever my father was, probably. The next day, my father acted as though nothing had happened and asked me to invite my friend to Blackpool for the evening. We all went, and we were all treated to a pretty good night, went on a couple of rides, had some food and went into the arcades.

Again, it was one extreme to another; there was no in-between with the guy. He would be a typical example of Dr Jekyll and Mr Hyde. Father was always good at doing stuff like that. A raging lunatic one day and the next day he would come across as a loving family man.

My father, in a way, was two different people completely. The way he was indoors was someone to fear; it always felt as if you were walking on egg shells, too scared to step on a crack, wouldn't talk in case you said something wrong or something that would upset the inner monster of him. I would only talk when I was spoken to; it was easier to give one-word answers. In a way he was really clever because as I was growing up and witnessing what he was capable of, knowing that at a flick of a switch you could get a beating or witness him smashing the house or beating your mother till she was black and blue – yes, he was clever putting the fear in you from such a young age never to go against him or else there would be trouble. By growing up in such an environment you were too scared to speak out and tell someone. Outside the house he was completely different; he would come across as a good family man. He would take me as well as other kids from our area into the nearby fields with our dirt bike and let everyone go on it; it was as if he wanted to be liked and loved by everyone around him. I think he loved the attention of the neighboring kids, being looked up to as an equal really. To be fair, we did have a lot as kids, we had the newest quad bikes that were out, and as we got older, we always had the newest off-road dirt bikes as well as other stuff. But as I sit here and think about all that I start to wonder: was it all for show? What looks good on the outside covers up what is really going on indoors.

As I said, there were two different people to my father, but in his way, he did a lot as well but by breaking the law alongside my mother. As I was growing up my mother never worked a day in her life until I was sixteen. So she was on benefits, got income support, housing benefit and council tax benefit. She was making out that she was a single mother living on her own. But the truth was even though she was getting all that money, she wasn't a single mother at all as she was living with my father in the same house and he was working full time. So the money was coming in; they had no rent to pay for or council tax, and she was getting a weekly income from her income support. On top of that you had my father's wages each month. So we always had nice cars, going on summer holidays abroad every year, then later on – I think I was around 12 – we started having two holidays; one was in the summer but we also started going away in the winter when my father got the taste for skiing. So in that aspect, sure I was lucky. I started to travel to different countries from the age of nine. But as I said earlier, was it only to cover over the cracks as to what was going on behind closed doors, or in his own twisted way was there a deep setting of guilt? Trying to make up for the wrongs that he had done, who knows, but if that was the case why then continue behaving in the same manner, never willing to change? He would want to change others, like: don't drink, you need to stop smoking, don't wear that etc. etc. Looking back at his behaving, I can clearly see that everything had to go his way and only his way; there was really never any compromise. If things didn't go his way, you could see him getting angry and then he would start being argumentative and then just lash out or start a fight. He would always make out that it was my mother that enjoyed waiting until the weekend to kick off and ruin his couple of days off work, but in truth it was him that always started the arguing; he could never let the little things go, he would just carry on and carry on until the worst case happened and he just started to lose his shit and hit out. Also, he was very clever at turning your way of thinking around to his way of thinking, so in the end you would actually believe that his way was the best; how he did it was unbelievable. I fell victim to that many times, when in truth nothing like that ever happened.

He was never faithful to my mother either. He had many affairs. The first one I remember was with one of the neighbors. I think she was some kind of student and she was having a house party. I can actually remember my mother sitting on the stairs with a glass to the wall and listening to him having sex with her. The neighbors' bedroom was next door to our stairs. I was only young, around the age of four or five, because my mother was pregnant. When he got back in after doing whatever he was doing, I do recall her confronting him. Next thing I heard was my mother screaming and I went downstairs to see if she was okay. What I witnessed was my father kicking her in the stomach and punching her, calling her names; it was awful. I don't know what happened afterwards, but I know that she was taken into hospital. Not long after that there was another girl who he actually left my mother for, but he was back home within a matter of weeks. There were quite a few and probably more that I don't know about.

I do have some happy memories in my childhood; it wasn't all bad, more so when I was away from the house and away from my parents. I loved going to school and actually enjoyed going as it was me escaping and I could lose myself elsewhere. I never had birthday parties or had friends around for sleepovers, and I only had a few around to have tea. On the plus side I was allowed to go to my friends to sleep over, especially when I was in high school, and boy, did I love it. Also, I was part of a running club, which I loved. I wasn't the best of runners but I was good. I was allowed to join the local Harriers club after I won a big cross-country race in the last year of primary school. I don't know how many kids were running that race. There were quite a few schools that partook in the event, and after the first big hill I led from the start really; both my parents were there to cheer me on. As I was getting closer to the end, I do remember my father running along beside me cheering me on saying, "Come on, you can do it, just dig in, you're nearly there, the end is close." I couldn't believe it when I won. The medal was in a case and I was so proud of myself. My parents, to be fair, were so proud of me too; it gave them something to tell their mates, especially my father – he went to work telling all his colleagues that I won, and one of his close mates gave him a badge to give me; it was of the Olympic rings. It was my father, actually, that put it into my head that maybe I could run in the Olympics in the future and it was something that I really wanted to achieve. So that was the start of my running competitions and that's when my parents let me join the local Harriers club. I ran for my high school in the cross-countries, always partook in the yearly athletics, both field and track, and I always won the yearly trophies apart from the last year of high school.

I was always secretive when it came to boyfriends. I wouldn't tell anyone at home, not that I had many boyfriends, to be fair. It wasn't as if I was the prettiest of girls or the most popular. I had a few friends, not many, as I found it hard to trust. To be fair, I think that part of me was kind of myself but there was always a part of me that always seemed to put a front on. I had arguments and fights, I was bullied in the first couple of years of high school. In the final parts of high school, I guess I became the bully, which I am not proud of. There is always a negative to a positive, as the saying goes. Thinking back to those times, I think I became a bully because of what was going on in my home life but also to show the ones that were bullying me that I wasn't as soft as people made me out to be. I just got so sick and tired of being pushed around and being picked on by the popular girls and the ones that were so street-wise and so cool that I started picking on ones who were so mild tempered and I knew I could push them around, just to make myself feel good and to show others: hey, look at me, I'm just as cool as you. To all those girls that I did do that to I want to say sorry to you all; it was uncalled for, and no matter what I was going through there is no excuse for that kind of behavior. Actually, there are a few lads that I was bitch to as well, for no real good reason apart from a couple of them were being dicks. I would just walk up to them, get as close as I could and I would just headbutt them as hard as I could and walk away. I don't know why I behaved as I did at times. I guess I wanted to show that I wasn't a walkover and that I had a backbone, or the fact that I wanted other kids to see that you shouldn't mess with me.

The problem with the negative thinking did start at home with my father, as I was at times picked on by some of the neighboring kids. I was socially awkward as a child and as a teenager, always struggled to know what to say to others; lads

I seemed to get on with better than girls, I guess. It's still the same today. I have more male mates than I do female. Anyway, slightly going off course, when this started, I would always run past them or if I had seen them before they saw me, I would walk in a different direction. Well, my father picked up on this and he would start the name calling, telling me I had "mug" written on my head, or I needed to grow a backbone, or I was spineless and I needed to grow a pair. None of this helped the situation; it just made me crawl within myself. That was until one day I just snapped and I had my first proper fight, actually outside my house. There was this girl who lived up the road from us. We were friends when she first moved to the area, but something happened; I cannot remember what it was. We just stopped hanging out and her attitude towards me just u-turned 180 degrees, she started getting cocky with me and the name calling started. One day she started saying something to me. I cannot recall how it started, but I told someone to push her into me which they did, and I just went for her. We were fighting on the small green in front of the house. I knew my parents were watching from the window as I heard someone shout it. I just lost control and I think I did some damage to her neck because she was walking back home crying and holding her head up with one hand and with the other, she was holding her neck. My father after about five minutes shouted for me to go in and he wanted to know what had happened As I was telling him there was a knock on the front door and it was the girl's father starting to shout his mouth off to my father. I was still boiling from the fight and I went to the door, pushed my father to one side and had a go at the guy. I was telling him that I had enough of his daughter's attitude towards me and in fact it was she that started by running her mouth. He actually raised his arm as if he was going to hit me, so with all the strength that I could manage I pushed him with both arms and he stumbled backwards. In response he said to me, "You'll be sorry for that" and he walked away. About an hour or so afterwards there was another knock on the door and it was the police; the girl's father had called them out and informed them that I was a troublemaker and I had started on his daughter, so the police wanted to hear the story from my point of view. Luckily, there was no further action taken by the police. I was given a telling-off, and that was it. I did feel bad the following day, though, because I saw the girl and she must have gone to the hospital because she was wearing a neck brace supporting her neck. She never picked on me again and when we saw each other we were always pleasant, saying hello, and how are you etc., etc.?

I cannot say I never had another fight after that day, because I would be lying and that wouldn't be right for me to do. What I can say is that I never hurt another person like that again. The only fights I had, were the ones I got called out on and always out of school where no adults were around. I would show up scared shitless but I always followed through with it as I didn't want to come across as a chicken. I won a few but I also lost a few too.

I was a bit of a cocky bitch and always shouted my mouth off in the wrong sense and in the wrong place and it was that that got me in the shit. In a way I think it was me crying out for attention but the wrong kind of attention. You will understand this as you will later read how things got worse for me at home. I would do all sorts just to be seen or heard. I wanted to be the best, whether that was with my running, reading out in English, being centre of attention in drama.

Whatever I could do to be heard I would do it. I wanted to

be one of the cool kids and at the age of fourteen or fifteen I started smoking in the girls' toilets, which later had an effect on my running. I would leave school at dinner, started swearing more, all the common signs that I wasn't happy, but I hid it so well. All these changes started in the last two years of high school. I just lost all interest with everything; my work was going downhill, when I used to take such pride in it. My levels were going down; I started to answer the teachers back for no reason. However, when there was a chance for me to partake in something after school, it was always something to do with PE as this was my favorite subject. I would stay behind, anything to keep me from going home.

Chapter 4

The summer of 1996 I was fourteen years old. I was in my parents' bedroom watching a film, which we did on many occasions. I on this one occasion had fallen asleep on my parents' bed. At some point through the night I had ended up on my father's side of the bed. I remember waking up to this feeling between my legs, and it was my father's hand down my shorts and his finger was playing with my private parts. I was so shocked that I took his hand away and let it drop. He then had his hand on my left breast. I got up straight away from the bed and went straight into my bedroom and into my own bed. I never mentioned it to anyone. The following day whilst my father was in the back garden mowing the lawn, my mother asked me to go to the garage to get some milk or something like that. I left via the back-garden gate. On my return, as I closed the garden gate my father was there. When there was no-one in earshot, he said to me, "You're more mature and grown up than I give you credit for." At that time, I wasn't exactly sure or understood what he meant.

I do remember as a young girl when my father used to play with us, I would at times jump on his back and I do recall that he would put his hands on my bottom and he would squeeze it.

Now this is where it starts to get especially difficult. That same summer of 1996 my father tried to have sex with me. I recall that we had all stayed up late and when we were all getting ready for bed, my father told my mother to go on up. My father said that he was going to stay downstairs and make sure that everything was switched off in the kitchen. He asked me to double check that everything had been switched off at the wall in the living room, which I did; it was quite dark in the room as the lights were all turned off. My father came into the room. I remember him walking towards me and me walking backwards. He put his hands around my waist and I ended up on the sofa. He went onto his knees and pulled me further towards him, so I was on my back on the sofa and my legs over the edge. He started pulling my underwear down. I started to cry and asked him not to do it; he completely ignored me and continued doing what he was doing. I was petrified as he was lowering his own tracksuit bottoms and underwear. He got me further onto my back and positioned me so I was on the same level as him. I tried to grab hold of my knickers, but he grabbed me by my wrists and held my arms above my head. With his other hand he completely removed my knickers. I asked him to please stop, to let me go, and then I felt it. He started to penetrate me with his penis. I cried out as it was incredibly painful and sore. Again, I asked him, "It hurts, please stop, I don't want you to do this, it hurts, please stop it."

He put his hand over my mouth and said to me, "We don't want to wake anyone up and find us, do we?"

I couldn't stop crying from the pain. I said no, please don't do this. I asked him to stop but he just continued to try and penetrate me. Then he gave me this look that terrified me and he answered back saying, "What's wrong with you, all girls your age are having sex, don't be so fucking soft."

In response I told him again, "Please no, I don't want this, just let me go."

After I said this, he let me go. I grabbed my underwear and ran upstairs to the bathroom. He hadn't fully inserted me, just partly. I remember seeing some blood on the toilet paper like a spotting. I left the bathroom and there he was standing on the top step giving me an awful grin and a look. I just went past him without saying a word and went straight to my bedroom and I silently cried in bed. I never told anyone as I was too scared, scared of my father as I knew what he was capable of, scared of not being believed, so I just kept quiet.

After that incident the following month we went away on our yearly family holiday to Menorca. I can recall that on one occasion, which was in the second week of our holiday, my father again for the second time forced himself on me. We had a two-bedroom apartment; my parents were in the big double bedroom, my grandmother was in the second and I was in the living room on the pull-out bed under the sofa. On this one night it was in the early hours as my grandma was in bed asleep and I thought my parents were too. My mother came from the bedroom into the living room and asked me to go into her and my father's bedroom. I cannot remember one hundred percent how it started; I just remember being there. My father was naked, and my mother was just in her underwear, but as she got under the covers, she took her bottoms off. Then they both started having sex with each other whilst I was there in the room watching it happen in front of my eyes. After about five minutes or so, it could have been shorter than that, I don't really know as time just seem to stand still, my father told me to lie on the bed next to my mother. I was wearing one of those long t-shirts that had that fringe design of the sleeves and the bottom of the shirt. I don't know if I had underwear on or not;

that bit is a bit fuzzy. After he got me to lie on the bed next to my mother, he started to part my legs and I looked at him in fear. I told him to stop, "Please no, stop this, I'm begging you, no, stop." My mother just got up from the bed and stood there in the corner of the room next to the bedside unit just watching, not saying anything, and I looked at her with fear, hoping that she would stop what was going on, but she never moved, never spoke; it was as if she was frozen. I was so scared my voice wasn't being heard, I was tensing up as I felt the pain of my father's penis trying to enter me, I just started crying, begging him to stop; all he said to me was, "Just relax and it will soon be over", but I couldn't; it was just too painful. All I could do was silently cry whilst he was above me giving me that terrifying look I knew so well. Then all of a sudden, I heard my mother's voice telling me to "relax". In response to her I cried and said, "I don't want to do this." After trying to penetrate me and failing to do so, he got my mother back on the bed and started with her again, just having sex in front of me as if it was the natural thing to do. There I was crying and in pain just wanting to get out of there, but I wasn't allowed; I had to stay. My father wouldn't let me out of that bedroom. It was as if he was on a mission and nothing was going to stop him from achieving it; he was already a monster, but there was an even bigger inner monster starting to come out. After having sex with my mother for the second time he got me back onto the bed and positioned me where he wanted me to be and all I could do was look at my mother, pleading with my eyes. She just looked right through me as though I wasn't there. No matter how hard he tried he was finding it difficult to penetrate me. I was crying, tensing up doing my best to make it as difficult as I could. He was getting frustrated; there was blood on the sheets all the while I was saying NO. Then out of nowhere my mother spoke up, she looked at me then at my father and said, "I'm going to the beach, I'll leave you two to it."

I silently cried out, "No, please don't go, don't leave me, I don't want to do this."

This seemed to anger my father. I don't know how long I was in that bedroom for; it must have been at least two hours or more even. My grandmother was sound asleep in the bedroom next door. He knew she wouldn't wake up because she always loved a drink on holiday in the evening whilst she enjoyed watching the evening entertainment. After a while and my father failing to get what he wanted from me, my mother told me to go back to bed in the sitting room. It was never mentioned or spoken about, and everyone just continued having a lovely holiday. I was distant for the rest of the holiday and always hung out with the friends that I had made during the day and in the evening.

A couple of months later, about two weeks after my fifteenth birthday, we all travelled up to Scotland to pay a visit to see my auntie and uncle (my mother's sister and her husband). They had invited us up to stay the weekend with them. I had a great time there and enjoyed catching up with my cousins and having fun. I loved the house that my auntie had; it was an old farmhouse in the middle of nowhere right in the Scottish countryside. So many beautiful views even in the autumn; you could look across the fields for miles. When it was time for us to leave, my aunt showed my parents this cutlery set. It looked really expensive and still in its box. All it needed was a good clean and shine. So my parents accepted it; I cannot remember if they paid for it or not or if it was a gift.

Anyway, once we were home and we had our tea, I was in the kitchen with my mother washing the pots and cleaning the kitchen, my father was upstairs in the small front bedroom polishing the cutlery, making it look like new again. He was up there a while before he shouted for me to come upstairs. I just thought that he might need my help or that he wanted me to take something up to him. So I went upstairs and asked, "Do you need anything?" just as I always did when he shouted. Once I was in the bedroom, he grabbed me and put me on the bed. He was so rough; my eyes welled up straight away and he could see the fear I was feeling but he just had that evil grin on his face as if nothing was going to stop him. He was harsh and fearful this time. He held my arms above my head again with more strength to his grip; with his other hand he roughly pulled down my bottoms and used his foot to remove them completely. He pulled his tracksuit bottoms down as well as underwear. He was forceful and hurtful when he was positioning me so that I was the right level for him and then with one hard thrust he penetrated me and had sexual intercourse with me. I can recall that my father had a smirk on his face and I will never forget the words he spoke to me. He told me at least he can say he had taken someone's virginity and I was no longer a virgin as I now belonged to him. I was in so much pain, I felt dirty and cheap and no amount of saying no to him changed anything; he wouldn't stop until he got what he wanted. Afterwards I went straight into the bathroom, sat on the toilet crying and I was bleeding once again. I couldn't run that bath fast enough just to get in and try and wash him away from me.

A few days later I was kept off school and my mother took me to the doctors. I had no idea why I was to attend an appointment as I wasn't ill, and there was nothing else wrong with me. So as we went into the doctor's room and sat down, I was asked why I was there. As I didn't know my mother answered for me. My mother told the doctor that I was getting to that age where I was having boyfriends and that she thought that I should go onto the contraceptive pill to be safe. The doctor then looked at me and asked, "Have you started having sex yet?" In response I kept quiet about what had been happening at home and said one little word, "No." The doctor gave me a prescription for the pill and we left the surgery. As my mother and I walked to the chemist to drop off the prescription and waited for it, I did notice that she was on the quiet side. She wasn't talkative on the walk there, and whilst waiting in the chemist it was as if she was in a daydream and again quiet on the walk back home. Once we were home, we had a bite to eat and sat in the living room watching TV. My mother was in her usual chair beside the window and for some reason I sat on the floor in front of her. The TV was put on silent and she started off a conversation with me, then suddenly out of nowhere she just came out with it, "Your dad has had sex with you, hasn't he?" I just broke down crying and told her everything. For the first time that I can remember my mother showed me some compassion, she held me in her arms whilst I cried and gently rocked me back and forth, telling me it was all going to be okay. I cried telling her, asking her that she needs to help, that I wasn't wanting to do it anymore. She gently told me to say no to him next time he tried anything or touched me, and not to worry as she will help me, and for the first time that I can actually remember she told me she loved me, and it will all be okay.

I would like to say that that was the end of the sexual

abuse/rape, but unfortunately it wasn't. My mother knew what was going on but she went back on her words to me. Instead of helping her daughter and protecting me, she turned a blind eye and played ignorant to what was going on right under her nose. The sexual abuse became a regular thing. It started happening every Sunday. My father would make sure that my mother would go to church every Sunday evening around six or seven o'clock and he would always make an excuse for me to stay behind; I needed a bath as it was school the next day, or that I had to go over my homework to make sure I had done everything the teacher had asked us to do. Mother never once said or asked, "Do you want to come with me?" She just did what father asked of her. The reason for her going to church was to do with me getting a free bus pass for the school bus or something like that, or free school dinners, I cannot exactly remember why, all I know is that because of the Christian high school I went to it was all linked to the church. My mother had to attend for a certain number of weeks. Right, getting back on track, I always had to get in the bath before they left the house, my father would go and drop my mother off at church and would always make it back as I was getting out of the tub. He would come into my bedroom and push me onto my bed and forcefully start having sex with me.

On a few occasions on Sunday evenings as it was all becoming like the norm, after my father came back from dropping my mother off at church, he started to get the video-recorder out to film himself having intercourse with me. Afterwards when he watched the recording back and he saw my reaction as he was abusing me, I recall him commenting, "You would think that I was raping you." He knew that I never wanted to have sex with him and I always said no; it was no wonder he said that to me because he could see my reactions. Not long after this he got me to perform oral sex on him. He was forceful, he wouldn't let go of my head and it came to a point where he was that rough that I ended up being physically sick whilst he was in my mouth. My mother knew what was going on back at home whilst she was away at church for those couple of hours. She would walk back sometimes and listen to what was going on at the front door with the letter box opened. Sometimes she would be pretending that she had forgotten her keys. I recall this because on a few occasions I was in the kitchen and I could hear as our letter box had a slight squeak to it when it closed. Then she would just come into the house and asked if everything was okay.

Chapter 5

All the way through me growing up as mentioned earlier there were always arguments in our household. When I was fifteen, I remember there were many more arguments happening, especially on Fridays, as my mother would go to the pub with my grandma. My father would get so frustrated if the housework had not been done or if they had been out all day. My father, as usual, would do what he did best, and that was to smash the house up or give my mother a beating. Things started to change, though, with my mother. Let's just say that she would do whatever she could to soften him, and if things were not going her way, then she had a back-up plan or a tool she could throw in to get him off her back. When the arguments were going on into the night, my mother would come into my bedroom to see if I was awake. If I wasn't, then she would wake me and tell me that my father wanted me. I would object and tell her I was too tired and I didn't want to go. In reply my mother would turn round to me and say, "It's you your father wants, not me." After saying this she would pull me out of my bed and start to drag me from my bedroom. I grabbed hold of my doorframe and cried to my mother, begging her, "Please, I don't want to go," but it was as if she turned off. Once I was in my parents' bedroom my mother closed the door behind me and she waited on the hallway landing. My father and now my mother were using me as a way to stop them from arguing. When I was in that bedroom of theirs my father took his frustration out on me and again forcefully had sex with me against my will. He would be rough and harsh, and there I was scared and terrified. My mother once said to me that she would help and if he tried to touch me again, then I must say no. When I did say no, it frustrated him; he would cause arguments and my mother used me as a pawn in a game to smooth him so that he was happy and good with her. After he had finished doing what he did to me he would let me go back to my bedroom, As I opened my parents' bedroom door there was my mother just stood there waiting on the hallway landing. She never looked at me. All that she did was go back into her bedroom and went back to bed with my father and went to sleep as though nothing had happened. My mother knew that I was crying. She heard me as I passed her. I went to my bedroom, closed the door, curled up in my bed and cried myself to sleep. It was never talked about. Even when my father was at work, she never brought it up. My own mother was now using me as a piece of meat. Whenever he lost his shit or started arguing I was used and abused in the worst way possible so he would get off my mother's back. This would, of course, happen quite often over time. I just couldn't see a way out of my situation.

I was fifteen years old when I attempted to run away from home because of the constant abuse I was suffering. It was mental, physical and now sexual abuse all at once, and I simply couldn't take any more. I went to my friend's house after school. I only mentioned a little of what was going on at home. I left the worst of it out. I told her about the physical abuse I was suffering at the hands of my father and that my mother would just stand by letting it happen. After I had my tea at her house, she asked her mum if I could also sleep over, but her mum said no, I couldn't that night. So on the way out and walking back towards where I lived, about fifteen minutes' walk, I said to my mate that there was no way I could go home, so she showed me a place close to hers in the woods where I could run to. I stayed there for a few hours but as nighttime came, I started to get scared and went back to my mate's house. As I walked up my mate's path to her front door her mum answered and she was actually on the phone to my mother, and she said to me, "It's your mum on the phone and they are worried about you."

In response I ran back down the path and shouted, "She isn't worried, she's an evil bitch."

Unknown to me my father was driving around areas to see if he could find me. As I was reaching the end of one road close to the local supermarket he drove past me, I heard his brakes being slapped on and he reversed the car back towards me, he opened the passenger side door to the car and told me to 'get the fuck in'. I just froze on the pavement as I didn't want to get into that car. He spoke again but this time he was more gentle, a little softer, "Look, just get into the car; we have been worried about you." So as I wasn't streetwise and had no idea what to do I got into the car and he drove home. When we had arrived home, my father got my mother to get on the phone to ring the police back and to let them know that they had found me. I had no idea that they had called the police out and reported me missing. I silently wondered if things might change at home after I did this. I also wondered if they were worried that I might start to talk. I felt sorry for my mate, though. I didn't half get her into a lot of trouble with her mum and she was grounded for trying to secretly help me. I don't think I ever thanked her for what she did for me, or actually said sorry for getting her into so much shit.

Things changed slightly at home but not for long. I think it lasted about two weeks, if that. It all started again after one weekend. I cannot recall the exact account of what had happened; what I can recall of the situation is I was downstairs watching something on television in the living room with my mother. The living room door was opened slightly, and my father was upstairs. He had been up there for a while, I don't know what doing. After a while I heard him coming downstairs and he just stood there looking through the gap of the door at me. Then suddenly he pulled this angry face at me and pointed to me, then pointed to upstairs. After doing this he went back upstairs and I just stayed in the living room watching what was on the TV. About half an hour had gone by and all of a sudden, he just starting shouting. It wasn't as if the shouting made any sense either. He just went on about: why does no-one ever listen to him and when he wants something it goes ignored. It just went on and on for ages, but I knew where it was leading to. It was about one o'clock in the morning and in comes my mother into my bedroom. This time she was crying, "Come on, it's you he wants, not me, he won't stop until you go to him." He got me lying on my front and put my head into the pillow so he could drown out my cries and just went hard into me, all his frustration being taken out on me with every thrust he did. He didn't care, he got what he wanted and he would have done almost anything like causing a huge row to get what he wanted. He was worse than a child having the worst and biggest tantrum and not stopping until someone gave in to them. That is the only way and best way to describe his behavior really, also I would call him as being satanic as well.

Spring of 1997. My grandmother wanted to take us on holiday. A lovely little caravan holiday for a week whilst on school Easter break. We went to a little place just outside Blackpool. It was a great destination to go to, especially for a teenager. It had both indoor and outdoor pool, evening entertainment for both young people and adults, and an amusement arcade. Both my parents spent the weekend with us and left Sunday night, as my father had work the following day. I was so happy as I loved spending time with my grandma and I was going to be away from my parents for the next five days. The only thing that was expected of me whilst being there was to call my parents through the week a couple of times. I made a few mates whilst there on holiday, and obviously I was distracted and spent a lot of time with my mates. My grandmother was okay with this, as at times she would encourage me to go out and make friends and have a good time as long as I was having fun and not getting into any trouble. The only thing that my grandma ever asked of me was to make sure that I told her whereabouts I was going to be and be back at the caravan at the time she stated. I did ring home. On the first time there was no answer and the second time I spoke to my mother. I think it was a Thursday evening and I was in the bar area with my mates on the dance floor. We were all dancing to Will Smith's *Men in Black* song. I was wearing black shorts with a pair of see-through pants and a white vest top. I had worn this outfit before on two different occasions with my parents going on family day outings. Anyway, slightly going off topic, on this evening I saw my mother coming into the room and she was walking towards me. As she was walking around the tables to get to the dance floor I recognized the look on her face. I looked over to where my grandmother was seated and there was my father speaking closely into my grandmother's ear; then he looked over in my direction and I could see anger in his eyes. Next thing my mother reached me and told me to go outside with her, as we approached the outside, she told me that I had to get into the car with her and wait for my father to come back. When we were in the car my mother said that my father was angry with me as I hadn't rung the house. I said to my mother, "Didn't you tell him that I had rung and I had spoken to you?"

"Yes, I did tell him," she replied back to me. To top it off my mother went on to say to me that my father wasn't happy with what I was wearing either.

I just stared back at her and cheekily said, "But you have let me wear it before without saying anything, why is now different?"

In her response she simply answered me, saying that the reason why it was different was because the times before I was with my father. What I got from that statement was that I could dress whatever way if I was with him; he must have got a kick out of it when other guys would look at me. When I wasn't with him, I had to then dress down? After my mother said this to me, I told her that I was scared and she now needed to say something to my father, tell him that she knew everything in regard to the sexual abuse and rape. What she went on to say mystified me. She said that she couldn't say anything to him now because she had known for too long, and if he found out that she had known all that time, then it would get her into deep crap with him. Instead her solution to all this was to keep quiet and she would make sure that he wouldn't go too hard on me, and she begged me to keep quiet to protect her as I knew what he would do to her. With that said she was right; I did know what he was capable of, so I protected my mother and kept quiet for her sake.

About twenty minutes later or thereabouts my father came back to the car. I was told that I was going home with my parents that night as I couldn't be trusted to stay with my grandmother. I have no idea what was said to her when they came to pick me up. I was accused in the car of being a lying bitch and that I was dressed as a common slut. My father said he should put me on the street corner the way I was dressed as men would pay money for girls dressed the way I was. When I didn't respond it made him even angrier and he just got louder and louder. He would speed up on the motorway whilst shouting questions at me. When I told the truth to the questions this made him even madder; because I wasn't answering the way he wanted me to he would threaten to crash on purpose. He would at high speed drive up to the back end of large vans or even lorries; I would scream out telling him to stop, please. He would angrily shout back at me, "Tell me what I want to hear." So the only conclusion I had was to lie and tell him what he wanted to hear. Once we were home my mother went straight upstairs into her bedroom and left my father with me. He grabbed me by my hair and dragged me into the living room and threw me onto the floor. He stood over me and kicked me really hard in my stomach and again in my lower back. Then he went onto his knees pulled me up slightly by my vest top and punched me in the face and broke my nose. The next thing I knew is him shouting at me, calling me a slag, slut and a tart, lots of different hurtful things. Then he ripped my pants apart and threw them across the room. I was terrified and scared. I hadn't seen him like this; he was getting worse as time was going by. He pulled me to my knees and ripped off my vest top, then he started lowering his pants. I noticed that he was aroused fully; he grabbed hold of my head via my hair and pulled me towards him. He just started to slap my face with his penis, whilst at the same time calling me all these horrible names. Suddenly he threw me to the floor for the second time, pulled off my shorts and knickers, placed me on my front and started to slap my bottom really hard; he must have smacked it around ten times. After he had finished doing this he grabbed my hips and raised my bottom in the air, he got behind me, grabbed my hair and pushed my head into the carpet, then slapped my backside once again, then roughly thrust his penis into me. All the time he was calling me all these nasty names, I felt as if I was being treated as someone would treat a prostitute.

The following day it was like a normal day. Father went to work, mother did the housework and I just wanted to stay in my bedroom. I was red raw from the previous night and in a lot of pain. I was angry with my mother. She wanted me to protect her but what was she prepared to do to protect me? The simple answer to this question was nothing; as long as she was fine then that was all that mattered to her, always putting herself first, regardless who she has to hurt in the process. When my father finished work, he took a bath and we all got ready to go back to my grandma at the caravan park for the last night. The excuse my parents gave my grandmother for taking me away was that my mother needed help at home with the housework as she felt a little under the weather. Once the evening came on that Friday I was told to dress up by my father and we all went to the bar as a family. By the time we arrived and got our table and drinks, my mates had noticed me, so they came over to ask me if I wanted to hang out with them. I never answered them as I didn't know what to say or if I was even allowed to go with them, as there were three girls and two boys, and my father didn't like the fact that I had male mates. When I never answered my father spoke up and said, "Cat got your tongue?" I just shook my head, signaling no. In response my father told me to go with my mates and just to let them know where I was, if we were going elsewhere then just inform them of my whereabouts. I just couldn't compute his logic or his way of thinking, as I was already doing this throughout the week with my grandmother. I kept as far away and stayed well away from my parents that night for as long as I could. I didn't want to be anywhere near them.

In the summer of 1997, it was a Sunday evening. My mother was out at church and I was at home as usual with my father. I was in the kitchen sat at the table with a cup of coffee, and my father sat down opposite me and he wanted to talk about something that was important, apparently. So we sat down and he dropped the bombshell on me. He came straight out with it, no sugar coating it or anything. He said, "You know that I'm not your real dad, don't you?"

I didn't know what to say to this. I just sat there quietly and let him continue telling me all the information. He told me my dad's name and that he went to school with my mother and that now my stepfather had come into my life when I was only eighteen months old. Then he told me something that I couldn't believe I was actually hearing. It was the reason why my mother and biological father's relationship failed and ended. Apparently, my mother had a small flat at the time and one night my biological father had come home early to find my mother having sex with another man. My biological father had kicked the guy out of the flat, then brutally attacked my mother, followed by him raping her. As this was going around in my head, so that I could make sense of it all, all I could think about was: well, isn't that exactly what you have done yourself to me? In his own sick twisted way is he using his own life experiences and making them out to be other people doing it? So that he can try to make sense of what is going on himself, who knows?

One Friday I hadn't cleaned my bedroom properly. To everyone else, well everyone that's normal, my bedroom was spotless. According to my stepfather I hadn't done a proper job at cleaning my room as there was a spot of dust behind my dressing table that I had missed. I suffered physical abuse at his hands. He got hold of the small hard plastic hand brush and hit me over the head, on my back, all over my arms; he just wouldn't stop hitting me. I would turn up to school covered with numerous bruises. I did speak up one time. I told another close friend and showed her my bruising on my arms and she encouraged me to speak to my form tutor. So after registration and the class went on their way to their lessons I stayed behind. I showed my form tutor all my markings and explained how I came to have them. She was so nice and patient and understanding; she said to leave it with her, she would have to inform the deputy headmaster. The Children's Services were called into school and wanted to talk to me. I had to give them the full account of what had happened, and the reason why I got such a punishment. I so wanted to tell them the full extent of what was going on at home but when I tried it was as if my tongue just froze. I couldn't actually get the words out to tell them, "I'm being sexually abused and raped." So I kept quiet and said nothing. The deputy headmaster told me to go to him once school had finished and he was to take me to the

Children's Services so that they can take me home. They wanted to talk to my mother to get her side of the events that had occurred. When I was taken home by a woman from the Children's Services, my mother looked a bit taken aback. As we went into the house my mother took the lady into the living room and I followed. When the question was put to my mother what had happened, she simply turned around and said that she had no idea that that had happened as she didn't hear anything as she was in the bath at the time. I just stared at her angry at her lies. Yet again her child comes second. She literally would throw anyone under the bus to protect herself. She was in the bedroom when I was given a beating. Once the lady left, I left straight away. I went to visit a builder friend that I was getting close to who was working on the nearby new superstore. I tried to open up to him once but found it to difficult, so I changed the subject. He was a good guy. We really liked each other. Nothing happened between us; he was having to go up north, I think in Scotland on another job, but would be back again in three months' time. He took my phone number so that he could keep in touch. I had to put an end to it pretty much straight away in one phone call. As I was talking to him on the phone my father was listening in on the upstairs telephone in his bedroom, and out of nowhere the guy actually said, "Is your dad listening in?" In response I said no. He wanted to meet up for a coffee and even said that I should bring my father along so he could introduce himself. This wasn't possible even if I wanted it to be, as you will find out later.

I did not know how to get out of this situation. Once the abuse started it was difficult to escape from it, especially when you have suffered in a way all your life. It just started to become the norm for me, as I didn't know anything different.

My mother and father acted as if this behavior towards me was normal. It was only later on in life I knew that I had lost all my childhood and teenage years to abuse.

Evidence found in the Children's Services reports…

The year 1997. It was reported to Children's Services via the headmaster of my high school. I had alleged that my father had hit me the previous night with a belt and a hand brush. That I had bruises on my arms and lumps on my head and forehead.

I had told my deputy headmaster that there had been some disagreement over a dressing table, and her father had hit her with a belt. She later tried to apologize and her dad hit her again with a hand brush and threw the hand brush at her. He then told her to say that she "wished him dead", and if she didn't, then he would kill her. He then made her sleep in the bathtub. The following morning, I went into school without any breakfast. I confirmed that I was too frightened to go home. Mrs Wells informed Mr Foster that she would speak to her manager and would come back to him later.

Mrs Wells was later instructed to pay a visit to the parents and then to speak to the girl (meaning me).

Mrs Wells came to see me with Mr Foster at school. I repeated what I had said to Mr Foster. It was visible to see that I was too frightened to go home. I was then told by Mrs Wells that they will get in touch with my parents, and that they will be there with me when they take me home. Where they will help to resolve this so that I wasn't in any danger.

Chapter 6

At the beginning of 1998 I hadn't long turned sixteen. I became pregnant with my stepfather's child. I was on the contraceptive pill at the time but occasionally, from time to time, I would forget to take it. As my pregnancy progressed and I couldn't hide it anymore as I was showing around five and a half months in, my mother and stepfather explained my pregnancy to others, saying that I had fallen pregnant by a builder who was working locally. The reason why they had used the builder that was at the time working locally, was because I had something there with him but hadn't taken that first step. He was the perfect cover story to hide who was really the father of my unborn child. After the phone call I only saw him once more; it was about two months later, I think. I was with my mother walking to the local supermarket and he was there with one of his colleagues. We both saw each other and I was very pregnant by now. After leaving the supermarket I went in a different direction as I was walking home on my own. I didn't want to bump into him and be made to answer any awkward questions. If I had bumped into him, I honestly think that I would have told him everything, and I mean everything.

During my pregnancy my mother and stepfather were being investigated by the benefits agency. I went into detail earlier on; well, all that cheating the benefit system had come and caught them both on the arse. Fifteen years that they had been living together, my stepfather working all that time in a really good and well-paid full-time job. Whilst my mother was claiming income support, as well as housing and council tax benefit as a single mother. It was really bad; my mother had to go to tribunal after tribunal and every time the verdict always went against her and my father. My mother then started to threaten them with taking her life as well as the life of her children, as she couldn't cope with the strain that the authorities from the benefits department were putting on her. They had stopped all her money and housing and council tax benefit, and they wouldn't allow my mother to have a food bank voucher. Don't get me wrong; both my parents fought all the way; they even got me involved in the situation. My father would do a rough copy of letters and I would have to rewrite them all out again as I wrote neater than my mother, apparently. I wrote so many bloody letters. My father went all the way as to write to the government commissioner in charge of the benefit department. Unbelievably, with all those letters my parents actually won their case and never had to pay a penny back. I thought the evidence was too strongly stacked up against them, but my father somehow managed to overthrow that evidence. It goes to show how clever and deviant he is, and he can be manipulative. My mother was forced to go back to work, which she did. Following getting a job she went on to buy the house about a month or two later.

Through all that stressful time there was many arguments between my parents and a few fights. There was one fight that got quite nasty and I was on the landing upstairs, and somehow, I ended up being involved in the disagreement. I think I was being used to take sides, which, of course, I refused to do. This made my father angry at me as I think he thought that I would take his side. I was around seven months pregnant and my father grabbed me and pushed me down the stairs. I recall crying out and I shouted up the stairs, "I'm pregnant." I wasn't allowed to visit my GP and I wasn't taken to the hospital to be checked out. Instead I had to wait until my next midwife visit and explained that I had a small slip on the stairs. As soon as I heard the heartbeat, I was relieved to know it was still a healthy heartbeat. When my child was born, when it came to the birth certificate, my name was in my stepfather's surname as I was brought up with this name, so my child had the same surname as me and my stepfather and when it came to the father's name being added onto the birth certificate it was left blank or father unknown.

During the year of 1999 I don't know how or when, but slowly things started to change in the home. The situation between me and my stepfather had somehow changed without me knowing. I was now being seen and treated as his partner overnight. At the age of seventeen I was now in a relationship with my stepfather and I didn't know how. The dynamics had changed also in the household. I was now sharing a room at the front of the house with my stepfather, my mother had moved into the back bedroom with one of my siblings, and another one of my siblings had the other small bedroom at the front of the house. I had now taken over the role of my mother, as it was now my job to cook all the meals, make sure the housework was all done, wash all the clothes. If I didn't do a proper job, then it was me that got a barrel of abuse.

One weekend, it was a Saturday if I remember correctly, my stepfather was cleaning his car and he turned around to me and told me that he had told his mother about us and that she wanted to meet me at our local pub that afternoon. I was so nervous about seeing her, as I didn't know what to expect, or what her reaction was going to be like. We had a lovely afternoon, to be fair. My grandmother didn't approve of the situation at all and she came up with a plan. The plan was that my grandfather should never know; I was to continue calling her grandma when my father wasn't around as I was always going to be her little girl, and I would only call her by her name in the presence of my stepfather. My grandma was quite open with me that afternoon and told me things that I had never known. Things that I am not going into as they aren't my secrets to share, and as she isn't here anymore it wouldn't be fair to write about them now.

Things were changing vastly and at a speed I couldn't control. Everything was getting out of hand and I had nowhere to escape to. I had no school, couldn't run to any of my school mates, I felt as though I had no-one. My mother was happier than she had been for a long time. It was as if she was living her life for the first time; she was finally free to do what she wanted to do. I noticed that she was dressing differently, wearing makeup, which she never did. She was happy and came out of her shell. Here I was getting trapped further and further. In truth it felt as if I was a caged animal that had been controlled and manipulated from being a baby, and that controlling behavior was my life. I had nothing: no money, no savings, the only things I had to my name were the clothes I had in my wardrobe, and I had no-one to depend on but my stepfather. I think that he totally knew this and probably he thought that this gave him the upper hand.

In 1999 I fell pregnant again with my second child to my stepfather. Once again when the child was born and it came to register the birth, I went down on the birth certificate using my stepfather's family surname as this was the name I was brought up with. The child too was given the same surname as myself, and under father's name it was left blank or father unknown. He never once wanted his name linked or known on any paperwork. He always wanted his identity kept a secret, but he was clever too, in a sense. The reason why I say this is because with me already having his surname growing up, I was known by that name throughout primary and high school, friends and family and when I was in hospital. So when it came to putting the children's names on the birth certificates, even though they were put in my surname, and the father was unknown, in reality they had been registered in their father's name. As I said, he was clever.

Sexually, things had increased with my stepfather. He was getting obsessed with it, and I was hating it more and more. I would be at home doing the role that my mother used to do, which was to keep house and have the meals made. My stepfather would be at work and my mother was now out working after her benefits were stopped. Whilst I was at home cleaning or doing whatever I was doing depending on the day, but I would think to myself, I'm sorry to say, that I wished he wouldn't return home. I actually remember thinking to myself, "I wish something would happen to him at work, I wish he would be involved in a crash or something or anything to prevent him from ever coming home." Well, anyway, my stepfather would start to come home during his lunch break for him to have sexual intercourse with me and straight after he would be gone and returned back to work. I had just given up; behind closed doors I was like a lifeless human robot. I was living the film *Groundhog Day* every single day, and all the

75

while I was slowly dying inside. I went along with the situation at home because, to be honest, it was easier to, and I was too scared of him to do anything else. I knew what he was capable of and how violent he could be and I was frightened that he would get physically abusive with me for objecting.

At the back end of 2000 my stepfather surprised me with a holiday. I had no idea about it and was shocked, to say the least, when a couple of days before we were to depart, I was told by him to pack a suitcase as we were going away. His behavior was slowly changing, it seemed to me, at the time as if he was mellowing, changing for the better, maybe. I was excited to be getting away, to be fair, as I loved travelling and experiencing new places. I hadn't a clue to where we were going, I had no idea what kind of clothes to pack even when I asked for ideas. I was told to pack as I would for the mild weather we have maybe in London. When we set off, I imagined that we were going away to some place nice for a few days in the UK, so I was totally surprised when we arrived at Manchester Airport. Once we were inside the airport and heading towards check-in, that's when I noticed on the display board that we were travelling to JFK Airport. I couldn't believe I was going to New York City, one of the places in the world that I have always wanted to go.

Once we had arrived in New York we caught a cab to get ourselves to the hotel. We were staying in the Carlton Hotel on the corner of Madison Av and 54th Street. I can't really recall the exact number of the street. We did all the touristy things like going up to the top of the Empire State Building; we went to a Broadway show and watched *Saturday Night Fever*. I feel extremely lucky to say that I went to the top of the twin towers eleven months before they went down. Last, and not least, we went to the top into her crown of the Statue of Liberty. The queues going up the Statue of Liberty were enormous, a lot of security also; they had bag scanners as well. I remember my stepfather getting frustrated when he had to empty his rucksack; he told me just to go on and he would catch me up. I don't know what it was, but I started to have this churning going on in the pit of my stomach; I could sense that something was going to happen, but I couldn't put my finger on it. Once my stepfather had caught up with me and we were slowly climbing up the stairs, as we were getting closer and closer to her crown the pit in my stomach was getting worse and worse. It was getting to a point where I had to sit on the stairs and get myself right, as I was getting hot and clammy and I was starting to feel sick. The sense that something was going to happen was intensifying. I wanted to get out of there so much but I couldn't.

Once we had reached the crown part of the Statue of Liberty we looked out through the windows at the view, and it was breathtaking. My stepfather was behind me looking in his rucksack for something. I just thought he was looking for the camera to take some pictures. When I turned around to see what he was doing, he was on one knee holding a box with an engagement ring. I was so shocked. I knew something was going to happen, but this? In my head I'm going, "Oh fuck, how am I to get out of this?" There were now people surrounding us waiting for my answer; in my head I wanted to say no. The reality of it, though, was different. If I said no to him in front of all these people, not only would it make him angry but I would have humiliated him in front of a crowd of strangers. Also, I had nowhere to go and run to, as other ones may have had. They could fly back home to their parents' house; I couldn't do this, as I was living at home and here with someone who in my eyes was still my parent. I was in a lose-lose situation. So I gave the only answer I could; I said yes.

So here I was engaged to a man that brought me up as his own, who I still saw as a father. I was engaged to be married to a man I hated and didn't love and all I could do was silently cry internally. The darkness was getting blacker and blacker. I was getting dragged in deeper to my stepfather's control. The longer this went on for the harder it was for me to get out and away from him.

In September 2001 sadly we lost my grandma. She was my stepfather's mother. It was so sudden and came as a huge shock for everyone that knew her. My grandmother was the life and soul of a party, she enjoyed going out and having a drink, she enjoyed having a smoke. Simply she just enjoyed life. I think her favourite place was in Menorca. There was this one bar she loved the most. The bar was at the top of an indoor shopping market that went upwards in a spiral. Once you got to the top you were outside; there were tables and chairs like a beer garden, music was being played outside from the pub. Grandma just loved it there. It was the perfect place to watch the sun setting.

After my grandmother's funeral, the big question was what was to be done with her house. As the house belonged to the housing association, my stepfather didn't want any strangers living in her house. Plus, my granddad's ashes were buried in the front garden as well as my grandma's dogs. My name had been on the housing list since 2000. My stepfather's idea was for me to ring the housing association up and explain the situation with my grandmother's house and if possible, if I was near the top of the list, could I be considered for the house, or something like that? As it was my name was actually at the top and my grandmother's house was going to be offered to me.

My stepfather saw this as a perfect solution to the living dynamics in our household. When I signed for the house and the house was in my name, I got the keys. My stepfather had taken my mother out and talked to her about an idea he had. I was kept in the dark until he had arrived home with my mother and they were looking happy and pleased with themselves. My stepfather's great solution was that my mother was to move into my grandmother's house and I was to stay at home with him, and that is what happened. I couldn't understand this; why would my mother move out of a house that she was buying and paying for the mortgage, and move into a house that wasn't hers but was mine? Why did she allow my stepfather to boot her out of the house and him to live there rent free? I couldn't understand, and I still cannot understand it till this day. My mother for the first time had the upper hand on him. She could have said no and kicked him out the house. She was in a new relationship and not long had a baby. I could have moved into my grandmother's house and be free of him, finally having my own space. Instead he still had a massive hold of her, and she would still do whatever he asked of her. They were still sleeping together, as I found out later; maybe that was the hold he had, who knows? So that was my mother – at long last she was in a way finally free of my stepfather; that was the final step, moving out the house and leaving the rest of us.

Later that same year my stepfather was made redundant from his job that he had been with for just over twenty years;

he got quite a big settlement from his employers. He could, though, have kept his job, but that meant that he would have to move to a different depot, or he could take the money and do something else. In the end he did take the money as he was tired of the shift pattern and working for other people; he wanted to be his own boss and start up his own business. Now that he had this money he could actually get started, but he had no idea what to do. It was I myself who came up with an idea and he thought that it was great. So he set up an airport travel service, and to be fair, it took off really well. My stepfather had business cards put into all the travel agents. He had an advert put into the local yellow pages. We were getting customers by word of mouth too. Finally, he had a good business of his own as he always wanted. Once that had become a success, in a way, it didn't need all his attention, so he was looking elsewhere wanting to try something new for a hobby.

My stepfather had always had a fascination with guns since I could remember. When I was a little girl, there was one night when my mother's brother and his best mate, I think, had been round at ours. It was nighttime and I was in bed when suddenly I heard a gunshot. It came from downstairs outside our front door. I could hear my uncle cry out, then my stepfather made hush noises. Then I heard him say that we needed to hide the gun. All that I can remember of that event was my mother quickly coming into the back bedroom getting me off the floor and putting me in the bed in the small front bedroom. The gun was thrown into the nearby park or river, and the police arrived at our house and went right through the property to look for the gun. I think that my uncle and father had been messing around with the gun and my father had fired the gun and it grazed my uncle.

There was another occasion that I have later heard about. It was when my stepfather had started to see my mother and there was one night that apparently, he had arrived at my mother's flat and threatened my biological father with a shotgun. Apparently, he was telling my biological father to leave my mother and myself alone, and if he didn't, he threatened to shoot him. Now I don't know if there is any truth in that or not as I heard it by word of mouth by a family member on my mother's side.

So with his fascination for guns he wanted to take it up as a hobby. He applied for a gun licence, which he was approved for. The first gun he bought was a shotgun as he wanted to take up clay pigeon shooting. I would also go along and sometimes partake. That gun was followed by him purchasing a sniper rifle, which he would take to the firing range. I think that was at a local army field where people could go to use their weapons and use their target range. Then he went on to purchase another shotgun, followed by a Glock handgun, where he would go to an indoor shooting range. He set up in the small bedroom at the front of the house a gun cabinet, so the guns were safely locked away.

It was New Year's Eve night and we were going out to celebrate the new year with my mother and her partner. It was a good night. I had quite a bit to drink and there was some of my mates there that night, and me and my mother were mainly on the dance floor all night dancing away. I didn't want to leave the hotel when it was time to go. Well, this obviously angered my stepfather to no ends. When we had got home, I was accused of flirting with other lads, and that I had made a fool of myself. When, in fact, the only lad I had spoken to was my mother's partner, and I definitely hadn't made a fool of myself. I had, though, gone into the other function room with a couple of girl mates and was just talking for a little while. Next my stepfather was accusing me of ignoring him all night, as if I didn't want him to be there. Truth be told, no, I didn't want to be there with him. I wanted to be free of him and his control. I had also started to answer him back and started to get cheeky with him, especially when I had been drinking, as it made me feel braver. I spoke up more and stood my ground even if it did get me into more shit with him, but I noticed that when I did this, especially in drink, it would infuriate him. As if I was speaking out of turn and that needed to be corrected by him. Well, on this occasion I actually thought he was going to kill me.

It was when we had got back in from the New Year's Eve party and he just wouldn't let it go; he was shouting and trying to cause an argument and he just wouldn't let it go. I don't know if it annoyed him if I kept quiet and didn't answer back, because when I was quiet, he would just carry it on and on and on until I finally snapped. This is want happened on this night. I was being accused of so many things and I was in the bathroom on the toilet when he accused me of wanting to shag around or something like that, and that was never me and he knew that. I remember shouting back at him through the bathroom door, "How can you say that when you know what you did to me, and you know that you were the first?" Then stupidly, without thinking, because I was drunk, I shouted, "Are you going to get your gun out?" I have no idea why I said this. I guess I was just fed up. I didn't want to be there. I never asked for this situation I was in; I was forced into something I had no control over and it was now affecting me internally. He lost his temper and whilst I was on the toilet, he threw open the bathroom door and punched me with great force in the face; for the second time he had broken my nose. He went into the small bedroom at the front of the house and removed the sniper rifle from the gun cabinet and said to me he could use it if I wanted him to. I begged him to stop; he managed to do what he always did. He got you begging, saying how sorry you were, you were in the wrong. Which always made him in the right. It was as if he knew no wrong.

A few months later and we had a business call to see if we could pick up a very important person. He was a Bollywood actor. Apparently, there was going to be a Bollywood film to be made in our local area. After picking up this gentleman and driving him all the way back down to London, somehow my stepfather had secured a deal to be the personal driver for the actors whilst the film was being made. I think the filming went on for about four months or thereabouts. I went to a couple of the shootings and was asked to be an extra. After the filming had finished there was a wrap party and my stepfather had been invited to go along and he was allowed to bring me. At first, I felt really awkward as I didn't know anyone there. I did recognise some faces from tv, but still I felt awkward. So I was on the white wine to try to loosen me up and to help me relax a bit. There was a load of food that was put on, which I ate very little of. In hindsight, this was a mistake on my part; drinking on an empty stomach wasn't the wisest of ideas. After the restaurant we all went to a club in the town centre, and I was pretty hammered by now. I just started dancing on the dance floor finally enjoying myself, and there was this bloke I started to dance with, all harmless. As we were dancing I thought this bloke was going to pick me up, so regardless who was watching me I jumped up in his arms and he caught me and I bent my back backwards and put my hands on the floor and the bloke let go of my legs so I did a backwards handstand. Instead of landing on my feet I fell onto my arse.

Everyone around us was laughing. I got back up and started to dance again. There was a big group of us now on the dance floor cheering each other on. I think that had to be one of the best nights of my life, and I didn't care of the consequences that I knew I would have to face later on. All that mattered to me at that moment was having the best night ever. Before I left the club, I did, however, ask the bloke for his name.

The following days after that wrap party were rough. I had received a beating. I had a black eye, I had a few cuts and bruises on different parts of my body. I was coming to the part where I couldn't take any more. One afternoon whilst my stepfather was in the bath, I secretly went through his phone to see if he had the bloke's phone number from the party. I was so nervous going through his phone and trying to keep a conversation going so he wouldn't get suspicions.

Bingo! I had found the number. I quickly wrote it down on a scrap bit of paper and hid it. Afterwards I would ring and speak to Adam and he was happy for me to ring him. After a time of getting to know him and we were now mates, I started to confide in him about the truth of my situation at home. I told him that the man who he thought was my partner, was actually my stepfather. I eventually told him all the sordid details. Adam was understanding and listened without judgement. He would give me advice, and strongly advised me to leave. We kept in touch and he was always there if I just needed someone to talk to.

Following this incident, it was early summer, and we were all outside with mates having a few drinks and one of my neighbors was going to have a barbecue. We were invited, we said that we would go round once my stepfather had come back from an airport run he needed to pick up. However, when he got back home, he said to me, "What's for tea?" I explained that we had agreed to go round to the neighbors for a barbecue, but he argued back with me, saying that he had never agreed to this. He became so angry with me, he grabbed me and dragged me away from the kitchen window and punched me in the face so hard that he broke my tooth, half my tooth fell out of my mouth and there was blood inside my mouth. My stepfather just walked out of the kitchen without a word and went upstairs to have a bath. Whilst he was upstairs one of my mates came round to see if we were still coming round for a barbecue; she must have known something was wrong because she asked if I was all right. I very quickly told her I was and that she needed to go as I knew if my stepfather knew someone was round at the house it would anger him further. Around five minutes later he came down the stairs and he was so angry now. I was asked who that was at the door, so I told him the truth. He couldn't understand why I answered in the first place. I explained to him calmly the reason for me to answer the door was because they knew we were at home. This didn't help me as he got angrier and he ended up punching me again. This time it was hard enough that I was knocked to the floor. Whilst I was on the floor, he got on top of me and pinned me down, he placed his hands around my neck and squeezed hard. This made me lose consciousness. I remember regaining consciousness and then having another punch to my face which broke my nose once again. Then again, his hands were around my neck and for the second time he squeezed hard until I lost consciousness. When I came around the second time, I was on my own lying on the kitchen floor.

My stepfather was away doing an airport run and I was at home doing the housework, and for the first time ever I was in the hallway downstairs cleaning the floor. For some strange reason I stood still for a minute or two and looked around me and I thought to myself, is this it? Is this what my life is going to be like every day? Then I thought to myself: no, I want more, there is more to my life than this. I knew that I could not continue to live like this. I had to get away.

One weekday morning I was watching a television show, and it was discussing domestic violence and abuse victims, what help there was out there, and I sat down and listened to what they were saying. After finishing watching the show I set my plans in motion. I never used the house phone or my mobile number as calls could be traced. I used the local phone boxes and made arrangements with a women's refuge a few miles away. I was to get there two days later. I rang up a taxi firm, told them my details and to make sure my whereabouts couldn't be traced if my stepfather were to ring them. The last bit I had to do was to make sure that my stepfather was away from the house for a long period of time. So I made sure the day I had chosen he had an airport run on. What I did do, though, was make out that the flight was coming in half an hour earlier, to give me extra time just to be safe.

When the day arrived, I was so nervous in case I got caught out. Once my stepfather had left to do the airport run, I acted quickly. I packed up a suitcase as quick as I could, said goodbye to all my mates without telling them where I was going, but they knew I was leaving. The taxi came to pick us up and took us to the women's refuge. I was in Warrington for approximately a week before my stepfather used one of his family members to contact the refuge, who started to ask questions about me and my whereabouts and if I was staying at the refuge.

In order to stay protected the manager of the refuge thought it was crucial that we move immediately to another women's refuge. I thought of Adam at this time, and I thought that I would be safe in a refuge in his area. Plus, I also thought that if I was in a new place that I had never been to, at least I would know one person. So I was then placed in a women's refuge in Cumbria. The following day after the phone call I was taken to the train station and was seen off by the manager. So there we were, off to a different county to start off a new life.

Evidence that I have managed to find in my Children's Services report...

Mother very distressed as all benefits have stopped. Evidence the benefits department have is that my mother has been living with her partner for the last ten years. Mother is threatening the suicide of herself and all three children. No money coming into the household apart from child benefit.

Poppy Harte informed the meeting with the authorities that an initial referral had come through a fraud investigation by the benefits agency. There had been a longstanding history of domestic violence problems within the household. During the fraud interviews mother had threatened to kill herself and the children.

Poppy Harte went on to explain that an incident had been reported. The sound of a door being broken down and sounds of an adult and a child which sounded like rape. After speaking to the family, they seemed to have closed ranks. There was no evidence and no other complaints; therefore, there was nothing either the police or social services could do.

Summer 2004, long story cut short. My father contacted the police to report me missing. I was eventually found in a refugee in the St Helens area. I had been spoken to and had made a historical sexual allegation at the hands of my stepfather. I went on to tell the police that from the age of two I was systematically abused by my stepfather. A visit to be confirmed to take a statement.

Chapter 7

So here I was on the train heading for a new start and a new life up in Cumbria. Whilst I was in Cumbria, I got in touch with Adam to inform him of where I was going to be living, as it wasn't that far from where he lived. Once I got off the train and headed out of the station, I looked around me and the first thing that came to my mind was that it felt like home. I got myself and my children into a taxi and headed for the refuge. I was getting a little worried on the journey to our new home, as I wasn't sure what kind of people we would be living with and what walks of life they too had come from. The taxi ride was only about five minutes from the train station to the refuge, so not that far from the town center. The staff there were waiting for our arrival and we were made welcome.

Straight away we were shown to our room where there were two bunk beds, wardrobes, drawers and a television. There were two big bathrooms that were shared. Downstairs there was a large lounge for all to share. In one corner there was a computer set up, in the bay window there were huge numbers of children's toys, in the opposite side there was a tv set with DVD player and DVDs that you could put on for the children. Along one side of the walls were a couple of bookshelves filled with different types of books, some for learning and others for general reading. In the center of the lounge there were three sofas that sat around a coffee table.

The kitchen was quite big for communal sharing; each room had its own cupboards for tinned and packet food, whilst the fridges and freezers were all shared. You all had your own sections in both. Towards the back of the refuge there was an outside yard and a playroom for any children that were living there.

After letting me settle in the first day and getting a good night's sleep, the following day was filled with paperwork that needed signing. Afterwards I had to talk to the manager about the reasons I was there, and I had to go into great detail and relive a lot of my past going as far back as a little girl. The two women that were there in the office just let me talk. Never did they interrupt me; they were really good at listening and only when I had finished talking, did they then start to talk to me. They wanted me to understand that they were there if I ever needed to talk, they helped me out with things I needed to do and informed people that I had moved. They also gave me advice on my options if I wanted to talk to anyone else. They had informed the police of where I was, as they were aware of the situation following my departure from Warrington. I was asked later if I was willing to speak to the police. In response I informed the staff member that yes, I was. So the manager rang the police to inform them that I was willing to speak. I was then asked to go into the office as there was a policewoman on the telephone who wanted to talk to me. The phone conversation was brief. She introduced herself to me; for the life of me I cannot recall her name. Once she introduced herself, she explained that she would like to come up to Cumbria and take a statement from me, to which I agreed. An appointment was made for her to come up, I think, a couple of days later.

In the meantime, I was starting to make friends with some of the girls living in the refuge, and I kept in touch with Adam and informed him of what was happening. It was good that I had him; I could ring him if I ever wanted to talk, which I did many times. Adam actually wanted to meet up with me the day after the policewoman was due to come up to Cumbria. I agreed, and I was looking forward to seeing him again as I hadn't seen him since the wrap party. Plus, it gave me something to look forward to, because I knew it was going to be rough giving my statement to the police.

A couple of days later, whilst waiting for the officer to arrive at the refuge, I was getting so nervous. The feeling in my stomach was turning to knots and I was getting anxious and feeling sick wondering if I could go through with it. My children were taken out for the morning so I could be alone with the officer. When she arrived, it was around half ten in the morning. We were allowed to use the office. We had a brew made and we got straight to it. It took a good couple of hours to get the statement down on paper. Once finished the officer informed me that once she gets back to the office, she will type up the statement, then send it to me to sign. I was also informed that I shouldn't feel pressured into signing the statement, because once that was signed and the ball got rolling it will get quite difficult. I was told of all the stages and what would happen when it goes to trial, how solicitors will be, especially the defense solicitors, how difficult it would be for me emotionally and physically. Impact on all the family and distress that it would cause to them. I was given a couple of days to think about it before I made up my mind. I was glad that I was meeting Adam the following day to discuss it with him.

So here I was walking to meet up with Adam at the pub we both agreed to meet at and he bought me my first ever pint of John Smiths, which I actually enjoyed. We discussed everything from the police officer's visit, my statement and all that I told her. He offered his viewpoints from an outsider looking in. He was keen to tell me of the challenges I would be facing and could I really put myself through that and could I put the children through that? Adam was so convincing, telling me that I have managed to get away from my stepfather and I was here to start a new life, why put myself through all that when instead I could finally get on with my life? To me it made sense and so with my decision made not to go ahead with the police statement and pressing charges, we got another drink and enjoyed the afternoon. Adam, though, was too happy, and I remember him going to the toilet a couple of times, but I never thought anything of it.

When I got back to the refuge later on that day I went into the office and informed them that I wasn't willing to press charges and I just wanted to move on. The police were later informed and wanted to talk to me, where I was made aware that if I ever wanted to pursue the charges at a later date when I felt strong enough to do, so then just get in contact and they would take it from there.

I remained in Cumbria for approximately six weeks before my stepfather found us again. I had no idea how he managed it or how he found out my new mobile number. He contacted me by phone, and he was so convincing; he was telling me that he was receiving counselling for his behavior and that he was a changed man. He went on to say that he was desperate to see the children and begged me not to take them away from him. Mentally he was breaking me down, he still had a hold of me and could still manipulate me. I allowed him to have the children one weekend. Adam collected the children from me and took them halfway to meet my stepfather. The same happened when the children were returned to me. I was left gutted and felt so bad as the children told me how much they missed their father and how they enjoyed seeing their friends again.

In August 2004 I made the hard decision to return to my family home. The refuge was no place for the children as there were a couple of girls that were taking hard drugs in their rooms; the swearing and the behavior wasn't good to be around. Plus, I believed my stepfather when he said that he was getting counselling and that he had changed his ways. So I agreed I would return home. To make me feel safer, he mentioned that Adam was going to be there for a while living with us. My return to the family home, however, only lasted for about three weeks. Despite my stepfather convincing me over the phone that he had changed, I very quickly learned that it was a complete lie. He never once attended a counselling session, nor had he seen one whilst I had been away. I realized he lied to me to make me come home with the children. To me thinking back now he would have done or said anything to get me home with the children, as it was them he wanted home, not me. The persona he adopted was slipping away day by day.

To make matters worse Adam had left. Once he was gone my stepfather was quick to show me messages between himself and Adam. Between the two they had worked together to make sure I wouldn't press charges. He went on to show me the messages that Adam had sent to him whilst he was in the pub with me in Cumbria. He sent messages whilst he was away at the toilet, saying, "We did it mate, she isn't going to press charges." I was in total shock that this guy that had helped me and been there for me was also being there for my stepfather. I hadn't seen it. I was played for a fool again. Following this my stepfather's controlling and manipulative behavior towards me had started again. I knew then he hadn't changed because he was showing signs of his previous behavior. It wouldn't be long until the physical abuse would start again. I felt that his intentions all along were to get the children back with him.

I felt that I needed to escape my stepfather once and for all. I didn't doubt that he would look after the children as he hadn't ever directly harmed them. As he had managed to find me not once but twice, in Warrington and again in Cumbria. I knew that as long as I had my children with me, he would never give up looking for us and finding us again. Life on a constant move, going from one refuge to another would not have been fair on the children. So the only way I could escape such a dangerous man who had nearly killed me before and who had held a gun to my head was to leave on my own and leave my children behind, with their father and one of my siblings who was living in the same house as them. I made my escape up to Scotland in August 2004.

It was with a heavy heart and extremely regrettable, but at that time I wasn't physically or mentally strong enough to fight my stepfather for my children. I only intended this to be for a few months until I was strong enough. I was so deflated by being at my stepfather's mercy for years, being physically, mentally and sexually abused all my life. I had my childhood and teenage years stolen from me. I did not know my own identity due to the environment that I grew up in. I was controlled by a manipulative, controlling and abusive man. I could not let this continue and that is why I fled on my own. Being in fear for your life and always having to look over your shoulder is not a nice feeling. This was the kind of person my stepfather is; he likes to put the fear into you, so you cower to him.

Whilst away in the first month I actually met someone who lived a short train ride away in Carlisle. It wasn't the best of starts, let's say, but I thought he was a nice guy and deep down he was. We met whilst I was having a drink in a pub with a couple of friends. He asked me out on a date and I agreed, so we arranged to meet up a couple of days later. I was kind of excited as I was getting ready for my date. I caught the train to Carlisle, and we spent a few hours together in a couple of pubs. Whilst talking I found out that he had not long come out of prison and was on tag. When asked what he had been in for, Tom was truthful and told me he had been caught with around ten ecstasy pills on him, and he was on tag for a further three months. I told him a little of my past, and bit by bit I would tell him a little bit more. Our dating progressed into a relationship. He was a party animal and I was entering into a world I had never been part of before.

The first hardcore drug I touched was cocaine. I was at Tom's where he was living at the time and he was there in the kitchen with this white powder on the kitchen surface. I recall him making small lines out of it with a credit card and using a twenty-pound note that he put up his nose and snorted up a line of coke. I remember being nervous in case he asked me if I wanted one. When he did ask me, I told him I had never taken drugs before, so he showed me what to do, telling me to breathe up my nose hard and fast so I get it all. So because I liked him and it was a new relationship, I got it into my head that it would please him, but more importantly, I didn't want to give him any reason to finish the relationship. So I started to be someone I wasn't. Plus, it did also make me forget the real world for a little while. Tom also introduced me to ecstasy. I remember the first time I took them. I was so nervous and on edge, as there had been a few cases in the news about young people dying of ecstasy tablets. Here I was willing to take the chance, to understand the feeling of what it was like, putting my life at risk. I guess I just wanted to be accepted and to fit in, again being someone I knew deep down, wasn't me. I wanted to escape. I only took ecstasy once, maybe twice more after that. Tom and his mates were mainly into the cocaine and speed scene. At house parties you could guarantee that there would be drugs, one or the other. If not, then Tom would ring a mate up and ask for a score. It would only be a weekend thing, whilst you were out at a club or a house party.

Two and a half months in I fell pregnant. I don't think that Tom believed me as he thought he couldn't have children as his previous girlfriends had never gotten pregnant. He would at times joke around saying that he fired blanks and he would laugh it off. Three months into dating Tom finished the relationship; my past was too much for him and, I guess, at times I was still living in the past. I was heartbroken. I had no idea what I did wrong or what I could do to make up with him. I started to go off the rails slightly, drinking a lot and always being in the pubs. A couple of weeks later I did see Tom in a pub and as he was coming out of the toilets. I quickly went up to him and told him that I wasn't pregnant and it had been a false alarm. He was grateful for me telling him and we went our separate ways. I was starting to be in the pubs morning, noon and night and drinking heavily. I just wanted to escape and not be part of the real world. I made mates with people I shouldn't have and whilst drinking I was looking for fights. I had all this built-up anger, shame and frustration and I couldn't find a way out. I ended up getting arrested once for fighting and had to stay in the cells overnight whilst I sobered up.

Things came to a head when the hostel I was staying in said I had to go. I had nowhere to go; I was about to be made homeless. So I rang my mother and broke down crying and told her everything. My mother rang up my grandparents, who were away in Spain as they had a place over there and told them my situation. About fifteen minutes had gone by and my mother rang me back. She told me to get the train back home and she and her partner would pick me up and I could stay with my grandparents for a while.

So in November of 2004, after being away for three or four months, once again I left Cumbria and came back to my home town in Lancashire and stayed at my grandparents' house. Once back and settled in, after about a week I got the strength to give my stepfather a call and I explained that for the moment I was staying with my grandparents and that I would like to see my children. My stepfather agreed to let me see the children and went on to say that they had a school assembly and asked if I would like to go. After I said that I would love to we agreed a time and place for him to pick me up. As I was leaving my grandparents' house, though, and walking to the bottom of the road, there parked up was my stepfather. I had no idea how he knew where my grandma and granddad's house was or where they lived. The only person who could have told him was my mother. So even though I was back in my home town and had I felt relieved that he had no way of knowing where I was, again this was taken away from me as he was there and could pop up at any time now. So he picked me up and we went to the children's school and watched them in the assembly. The children were so happy to see me there; the smiles that lit up on their faces I will always remember. As the children were happy to see me, I was allowed to go back to the house and spend some time with them. I can remember them showing some of their schoolwork that they had done and paintings and drawings. After a couple of hours my stepfather took me back to my grandparents' house. Before I left the car, I asked when I could see the children again and he informed me that he would be in touch. So I left the car and ran into the house without looking back.

Shortly after this event I realized that I had actually missed two periods, even though I had told Tom that I wasn't pregnant and that it had been a false alarm. I hadn't actually been to the doctors or taken a test to be a hundred percent sure if I was or wasn't, in fact, expecting. I guess I was upset with him for finishing with me as well as angry for the stupid pathetic excuse he used. So with that said I told him I wasn't pregnant. Anyway, once I noticed that I had missed two periods I went to the nearest health clinic with my cousin, explained my situation with the health professionals and took a pregnancy test there. After the long two minutes of waiting, the results were as clear as day; I was pregnant. I was so happy about the pregnancy. I remember giving my cigarettes to my cousin Lola and stopped smoking. I knew that the hardest job was yet to come and that was the big discussion I had to have with Tom. I had to man up now and be honest with him.

So later that evening I sat in my bedroom at my grandparents' house ready to make the telephone conversation. I was so nervous and sick that I had a ball of stress in the pit of my stomach. Tom answered on the third or fourth ring. We shared pleasantries, and it was nice. I realized how much I missed him. After a couple of minutes, I had to tell him. "Look, Tom, there is something that I need to tell you. I'm pregnant."

There were a few seconds of silence over the phone; then Tom asked, "Who is the father?"

In response to his question I told him that he was and that I made a mistake the first time around. I explained that I hadn't been to the doctors and I had made an assumption and I had been upset with him. To be fair to Tom, he took it all fairly well. He asked me to go up and see him and to bring proof that I was pregnant. I couldn't be mad at him for that. I actually understood why he wanted to see proof. If the shoe was on the other foot, I think I would have said the same. After my visit up to Cumbria we had a good talk and discussed everything that we needed to, and we got back together.

In December 2004, a few days later, my stepfather got in contact with me and asked me if I would like to spend the evening with him and the children. I agreed to this as I missed my children so much. I never agreed to spend time with him, just the children. So that evening I spent a few hours with the children and I put them to bed after reading them a bedtime story. Again, my stepfather took me back to my grandparents' and dropped me off. Before leaving the car, I was asked if I would like to go to the cinema to watch *The Polar Express* with the children and I agreed. Following that conversation, he just told me that he would be in touch.

Approximately one week later after the cinema, my stepfather came round to my grandparents' house and my grandmother invited him in. I asked my stepfather if I could have the children sleep over on Christmas Eve until the following afternoon on Christmas Day, to which he actually agreed in front of both my granddad and grandma and we were looking forward to it. My granddad even said that the children could stay in my room with me. My grandparents very rarely saw their grandchildren, so this was a big thing for them too. Following this discussion, my stepfather made a point of talking to my grandmother and stated that he wanted me back and that we should be a family. To my discomfort, my grandmother was agreeing to this line of conversation, saying to me in her kitchen, "When you have children together you need to stay as a family unit, and the only way you can do this is being together. It doesn't matter how your relationship came about now, all that is important is getting back together for the sake of the kids."

Well, this led to a massive argument between all of us. I ran upstairs to my bedroom to get away from everyone. Within seconds there was my stepfather coming straight into my room without knocking or asking if he could come in or not. He just would not shut up, he was coming out with all this stuff that he had come out with before. I just looked at him thinking to myself, "All you are doing is talking a load of shit, you are just repeating everything you have already said, you will say and do anything that will get you what you want." Well, it wasn't going to happen this time. Once the argument started to die down, I told him and everyone else that was part of the discussion that us getting back together would never happen, as I had a new partner up in Cumbria and I was pregnant with his child.

Christmas was approaching fast and I had all the Christmas presents in. Christmas Eve was upon us and I was so excited as the children were going to be with me soon, but Christmas Eve came and went and my stepfather never turned up with my children as was promised. I went to bed that night crying. I heard my granddad downstairs talking to my grandma saying, "Weren't the children meant to be here tonight?"

My grandma's response was, "Yes, that's probably why she hasn't come down." Amazing what you can hear through floorboards.

My stepfather didn't stick to his agreement. He ignored all the calls and messages I sent. I never did see the children over Christmas and I didn't get to give them their presents.

After the New Year there was a problem at my grandparents' house and an argument. I was accused of something that I hadn't even done. After I had argued with my granddad and pushed him verbally, he kicked me out of his house. Once again, I was homeless, pregnant and with no money. Tom couldn't put me up as he too was having to move out of the property he was living in with his nephew. So I went to the council and they put me in a bed and breakfast for the time being.

In January 2005 my stepfather finally got in contact with me over the phone and allowed me to see the children and to give them their Christmas presents. Before I left them to go home, I had a quiet word with my stepfather and I explained to him that I was returning to Cumbria to be with my boyfriend so he could be part of the pregnancy and I wouldn't be living in Preston anymore. I stated to him that I wanted to maintain regular contact with the children. January 2005 was the last time I saw my children or heard from them. I had, though, heard from my stepfather, who told me that he was going to India where he had met someone and would be taking the children with him. He informed me there and then that I wasn't to ring him anymore. Obviously, I ignored what he was asking of me. I rang him on a number of occasions on his mobile, which always seemed to go straight to voicemail.

Chapter 8

In Cumbria I was staying back in the hostel where I was before; yes, the one I had been kicked out of. I was allowed to stay there because of the fact that I was pregnant and the father lived in the area, so that was my connection to getting a house. My pregnancy was going well and I hadn't long found out that I was having a little girl. I was seeing Tom a few times a week and I had been introduced to his parents and his younger sister. Tom and his sister were party animals. Guaranteed they were always out partying at the weekends, well more so Tom was, as his sister was a hard worker and a manager, so some weekends she would have a quiet night in. The hostel I was staying in also had a house that they would trust to some residents. Myself and the other girls were allowed to move into the house, which was fantastic as it got me out of the hostel. Once I was living there it meant that Tom could sleep over, which was good for our relationship.

As our relationship was moving forward, I noticed that Tom would say that he would be over to mine on a Friday evening after being out with his mates. Well, Friday evening came and went, and he would most of the time never show up. Instead he would go back to his mate's house for a house party and take cocaine or speed. Once he had finished his session, instead of going back home to his parents' house where they would know that something was up with him, he would come to mine absolutely off his face to sleep it off. In fact, this was the only time he would stay over at mine, as he would always want me to sleep over at his parents' place, as he had all his home comforts there. Plus, his mother did everything for him and cooked all his meals.

His sister didn't take to me at first; plus, she was best mates with Tom's ex-girlfriend. Things changed, though, after one weekend. I was out doing some food shopping in the supermarket that she was manager of. As I was approaching the tills, I caught a glimpse of his sister who was also shopping as she was having a barbecue that day. Tom was invited but I wasn't. Anyhow, as I had finished bagging my food and paid for it, Tom's sister came up to me and said hi and asked if I wanted a lift home. I told her that I was okay, thanks. In the end Vanessa gave me a lift home, which I was so grateful for, as I was seven months pregnant. Once at mine she helped me with the bags of shopping and took them into the kitchen for me and she was so nice. As she went, I said, "Thanks for the lift and tell Tom to have a good time." With that she went back to hers and I went to unpacking my shopping and relaxing in front of the television.

The following week me and Tom were going away for a few days before the baby came. We were going down south to Warminster to visit my auntie and uncle and staying with them. They were the only members of my family that I ever introduced Tom to. We had a good time and it went by so quickly. My auntie had given us a pram and, I think, some clothes for the baby and, I think, some clothes for me. My uncle took Tom out to see Stonehenge whilst I went shopping with my aunt and my two baby cousins. We went to the working men's style club and had a few drinks, me on the soft drinks, obviously. All in all, it was a really good break for me, and I had a great time catching up with a part of my family. I don't feel, however, that Tom enjoyed himself much because he wasn't that engaging in conversation and would only communicate if any questions were directed at him. He just seemed uncomfortable the whole time we were down there.

On the day we were leaving Tom brightened up a bit. I, meanwhile, was a little upset that I was leaving them; the days just flew by. So I said goodbye to my uncle that morning before he went to work, and that afternoon my auntie drove us to the train station and we hugged each other good bye and promised to stay in touch. I promised that I would give her a ring once I was back home to inform her that I had got back safely. Once me and Tom were on the train heading back up north, he was becoming talkative again and had planned to meet up with his mates once back in Cumbria.

When back in Cumbria and outside the train station, Tom walked me to the taxi rank and helped me into the taxi with all my luggage and the pram that my auntie had given us and gave me a kiss goodbye and he went to meet his mates and went out clubbing. Once I had got home, I couldn't be bothered to give my auntie a ring, so instead I sent her a message just to let her know I was home safe and sound and thank you for a lovely time and we would talk soon. I then ran myself a bath and just soaked and relaxed. To be honest, I was tired and peed off with Tom and his behavior. Instead of saying anything I bottled it up and kept my opinions to myself. Now, though, I can say he was rude and standoffish from the word go. I noticed his behavior had changed as soon as we got on the train to make the journey south. He was miserable whilst we were down there. The only time that he was happy was whilst we were in the club having a drink, and on the train making the journey back up north. Knowing he was meeting up with the lads seemed to put a bounce in his step.

I never saw or heard from him until a day and a half later, when there was a knock on my door at four o'clock in the morning and he was totally off his head on both drink and drugs. He had been out, ended up at his sister's house, then back out to go clubbing followed by a house party at his mate's place. Obviously, his mate had called time on the get-together at his and Tom had nowhere else to go apart from coming to mine. His excuse for waking up his heavily pregnant girlfriend was he couldn't go home and let his parents see him like that. His parents didn't know that he was taking drugs, so he couldn't allow them to see him off his head, hence why he was waking me up at stupid o'clock.

Tom stayed at mine for a couple of days following that, and it was nice. One evening his nephew popped round with his dad. They had brought round some lagers and just started to have a session there in my living room that I was sharing with another girl from the hostel that the house belonged to, but because I loved him I didn't say anything when I knew I should have, and I just let them continue. After a couple of hours Tom went outside to make a phone call as he wanted another gram of cocaine and whilst he was out there on the phone arranging a pick-up, who showed up but the manager of the hostel and coming to do a house inspection. I was so nervous as I saw her through the window. I very quickly went round the living room with a friend and tried to hide everything and ran all the beer cans into the kitchen bin. I could tell that she wasn't happy as I still had to live by the rules as though I wasn't staying in the hostel itself, I wasn't allowed to have anyone at the house apart from Tom, and straight away she told his nephew and his mate to go and I was given a verbal warning.

Half an hour after she had left Tom's nephew Zach returned, and he had the cocaine on him. He came back into the house and he and Tom had a session. I tried to stay up but I was getting too tired and ended up going to bed. Woke up the following morning and Tom hadn't come up to bed; he and Zach had pulled an all-nighter downstairs in my and my mate's lounge. Why they had stayed at mine and not gone to his nephew's place I don't know. Thinking back on this event, I wonder to myself: was I being used? Anyway, the following day when their drug comedown started to kick in, they couldn't get their hands on any more coke, so as the comedowns were getting worse their only option was to have hair of the dog and start to drink. Well, as the day progressed and they were both drinking more, especially Zach – he was guzzling it down, they both started to get a bit loud and an argument came about. I was eight months pregnant and I was there sitting on the sofa when suddenly Zach pushed Tom in the heat of the argument and Tom landed right on me, on my stomach. Well, that was the worst thing that Zach could have done. Tom was in shock and the first thing he did was to make sure I was okay and no harm had come to me. Then he turned around and shouted at Zach, "What the fuck do you think you are doing? You could have hurt her and the baby."

Then in the blink of an eye Tom just went in on Zach and started punching him. The girl I was living with – she had her male mate there and he got hit by Tom's nephew Zach. Wrong place at the wrong time. He was okay, though. Next thing we know is that Tom is throwing Zach out the backdoor and told him, "Do one, that's it for me and you." That wasn't the end of it. Zach shouted some form of abuse at Tom and the next thing we know is Zach is kicking our backdoor in. He thoroughly kicked the bottom of the door right through. I had no idea how I was going to explain this to the hostel. Instead of worrying about it there and then, me and Tom went to his parents' place and stayed there for a couple of days. After a day I rang the hostel and spoke to the manager and made out that I had been out and I came back to the house to find the back door had been kicked through. I explained that I was going to stay with my boyfriend at his parents' house as I was too scared to stay there whilst the door was as it was. No more was ever mentioned about it and by the time I arrived back home the door had been fixed.

In June of 2005 Tom's grandmother had died, his dad's mother. So I went to support him and attended the funeral. I was so nervous meeting the rest of Tom's family, especially his younger sister, as we didn't get off to the best of starts. Considering it was a funeral there was a good turnout and everyone was having a good time. During the wake Tom's younger sister Vanessa called for me to sit next to her as she wanted to talk to me as we hadn't had much in the way of a proper conversation. Once the pleasantries were all over, she turned to me and said, "Can I ask you something personal?"

In response I simply said, "Sure, what is it?"

She just came straight out with it. "I hear that you already have children, is that right?"

So even though it wasn't the right place to discuss it, I told her the truth, "Yes, I do. Why, and who told you?"

Apparently, after Tom and Zach's fight, Zach had taken it upon himself to go round to certain people and share something so personal, that was my business to tell people when I was ready. When I told Tom later that evening, he just told me not to worry and he will have a word with his sister. As we both wanted to tell his parents about my past in our own time. Following the conversation with his sister she wanted us all to get together at the weekend so she could get to know me better.

So arrangements were made for the following weekend and everyone carried on with their night. After the wake of Tom's grandmother, everyone wanted to continue the party as they kept saying. So taxis were ordered and we all went to the working men's club in the town center. Tom's father came for about an hour or so and before he left, he left some money behind the bar for people to have some more drinks on him, and he went home with his wife. After a while everyone was merry and started to get a little loud and laughing a lot. Now when you cannot have a drink and you are in a room full of drunk people it can be pretty funny, and you can always see if trouble is going to start. Well, about an hour after Tom's parents had left, I saw him go outside on his phone. Half an hour later he asked if he could borrow twenty pounds off me and he got twenty off his sister. He went outside to a waiting car, got in for a couple of minutes and I knew he was getting cocaine. After that the night seemed to go downhill. Tom was in and out of the bathroom taking lines of cocaine as well as his sister. His sister's son somehow ended up drunk himself and got into an argument outside and ended up punching his fist though the church library next door to the working men's club. Next thing I knew Vanessa was wrapping her jacket around her son's hand to stop the bleeding and getting a taxi to take them both to the hospital. Whilst she was waiting for the taxi, she ended up shouting at Tom, because he was allowing her to go to the hospital on her own and he wasn't going with her. Tom was getting me a taxi to get me home on my own. He wasn't coming back with me because he wanted to go back to his mate's house to get higher than he already was. So what had started off as a funeral and wake turned into a night of piss-ups and drugs and a hospital visit.

Weeks came and went and I was getting fed up. It was a hot summer; my ankles were always swollen and I was in continuous pain with my back. I couldn't wait to give birth. My due date came and went. I had moved out of the shared house that was part of the hostel as I had my own house now through the housing association. I hadn't actually moved into it yet, though, as there was a lot of work to be done on it. So for the meantime I had moved into Tom's parents' place with him. Finally, nine days after my due date, I went into labor and I had a beautiful baby girl. Labor had been a dream from start to finish; it was two, maybe two and a half hours long. Tom was with me every step of the way. To be fair to him, he was fantastic; he held my hand and said soothing words to me. His mum was also there to give her support and she held my hand all the way through. I remember being shattered afterwards and recall Tom saying to me, "I'm so glad that you didn't swear with my mum being there." I just laughed as I didn't have a response to that comment.

I was in hospital for about two days or maybe a day and a half; it wasn't long at all. Vanessa came with Tom and the car seat to pick us both up from the hospital, as Vanessa had a car and Tom didn't, and she took the three of us home back to his parents' house. Once we had settled in at home, Tom and his sister went outside together whilst they had a smoke, and I could hear them having a conversation and his sister was being hard on him, telling him, "You need to sort yourself out now. If this doesn't change you, then nothing will."

When they both came back in Tom came out with a comment which made me look at him in shock; I was so taken aback. He said, "You don't need to question if she is mine as the poor thing has my nose." I never did bring it up with him later that day once everyone had left.

Later that same day I told Tom and his parents that I was going to give my mum a ring to inform her that she had a granddaughter. As Tom's parents kept asking when I was going to give my mother a call. As they still had no idea about my past, I had to keep the pretense up. Anyway, I did go outside the house and I did ring up my mother and let her know that I had given birth to baby girl. All she had to say was that she hated her name and gave me some names to consider calling her instead. I ended the phone conversation and that was the last time I spoke to my mother for a good few years. I kept that conversation to myself and never told a soul what she had to say, as I didn't want to upset anyone. The next step was going to be harder for me. I was going to write to my stepfather to inform him, as I thought it was important that the children knew they had a half-sister.

So in the middle of July 2005, I wrote a letter to my stepfather and to the children to see how they were doing. I gave the children my new address so they could get in contact with me if they wanted to and I informed them that they had a little sister. In the letter that I had sent to my stepfather I made it known that I wanted to see my children and asked my stepfather if this could happen. I also wanted the children to meet up with me so they could meet their little sister.

As you can probably guess, I never heard anything from

him or the children and this upset me a lot. I also knew that one of my children's birthdays was coming up in the August. Vanessa came up with a good idea one day and told me that when I send letters, birthday cards and Christmas cards, to send them recorded delivery and for me to keep the receipts to prove to the children later on if they came looking for me that I had thought about them and I did my best to contact them. So come August, I sent a birthday card with money inside. I sent it recorded delivery and I put my contact number in. Just in case when they opened it, they wanted to ring me up to thank me, or happy that their mother had remembered them and hadn't forgotten. I honestly thought I would hear from them but of course I never did.

Finally, I had moved into my own home. It was nothing spectacular; quite basic, to be honest. I was starting from nothing. Tom's parents allowed us to have quite a few things from his grandmother's flat after she died. The house had a few things inside but still the bare minimum. It was a typical two up two down house. We mainly lived in the bedroom for the first month. This was whilst we were waiting on the living room to be finished. We had a second-hand sofa being delivered from the housing shelter as that was all I could afford at the time. I did get a grant from the social but not very much, to be honest, enough to get paint for most of the house and bedding; oh, and enough money left to put down some cheap wooden floor for the living room.

I do recall from whatever money I had left Tom asked if he could have some to go out with, as he had arranged to go out with the lads. So me wanting to please him I gave him my bank card whilst I stayed at home with my daughter and I just spent the night chilling out. Tom didn't come home that Friday night or even the early hours of Saturday morning. I didn't hear from him until later Saturday evening. When he rang me to say he was at a house party at his mate's house and he wasn't coming back home that night either. His mate, I later found out, literally lived round the corner from us, about two minutes away. I was soft in the head with him because I just excepted his behavior without questioning him or wanting to rock the boat. I liked him and loved him at the time to put up with anything, as I didn't want to lose him. I think, looking back on that time, that maybe I was my own worst enemy. What I mean with this statement is I was changing to please the person, not letting him like me for me. All it was for me was making sure he was happy; that meant if he needed money, I would give it to him, no questions asked. Let him go out Friday and not see him until Sunday night without a word from him, even though he said he would only be going out for a few hours. Money he would want for drugs, go out and buy him his cans of lager. It was always about pleasing him because I didn't want him to have his head turned or drift away from me. By me acting like this and not being my true self because I still had no idea who I was, I hadn't discovered me yet, it had an effect on me mentally. The past was creeping up on me like the grim reaper; the black clouds from the deepest, darkest places of my traumatic past were taking hold of me. It was a recipe for disaster that would end with me at one of the worst breaking points in my life and my actions, as well as Tom's to a degree, would end our relationship.

Chapter 9

In December of 2005 after finishing work on Christmas Eve, I remember getting home and having a shower as we were going to Tom's sister's that evening as we were staying at hers for the Christmas period. Tom actually proposed to me before we left and I just recall me so happy as it was what I wanted. I was so over the moon I rang his mum and dad up straight away to let them know and they were both overjoyed for us both. After that I rang Vanessa up to let her know. In my opinion I felt that she was a little surprised by the news but wished us well and congratulated us. It was a good Christmas. I was becoming part of a family that I loved; my daughter was spoiled with an enormous number of gifts.

You know something? I thought getting that ring on my finger would have made me complete and happy, that it would put an end to all my insecurities with regard to Tom, and it did for a little while. We set a date for August 2006 which only gave us eight months to plan the wedding. The planning started off really well and I was really enjoying it, especially when it came to shopping for my wedding dress. I actually found my dress in January and it was the first one I tried on; the other dresses didn't seem to match that first one – I fell in love with it. The bridesmaids' dresses were being made separately. I had the flowers chosen in February and the venue was picked out in March. Once March was out of the way things started to get a bit hectic for me and I was stressing out a lot and I wasn't talking about how I was feeling with other people's opinions and decisions. I was starting to go along with what everyone else wanted. The color of the bridesmaids' dresses I wanted never came to be as Vanessa didn't want to wear that color. So I let her choose the color she wanted, and it was a color I never liked, but I smiled and pretended that yes, it was nice. She had to choose the style of dress she wanted to fit her body figure and wanted her breasts pushed up and on show. Things like this built up, but I just carried on. I started working a lot more. I think I was at work more than I was at home, to be fair. Also, I started to drink more and was getting stupidly drunk through the day on my days off.

I felt that me and Tom were becoming a bit distant and I remember on a few occasions when I was at home and I would sit back and watch him with our daughter: the closeness they had. I said to him a few times, "You can be so close to our little girl, but me, your fiancée and the mother of your child – you don't show me anything, you don't have that love for me. Why?" I was getting into a bad space in my head and I wonder now if the past trauma was slowing creeping up on me. I was back on the cocaine at weekends and drinking more heavily when my daughter was away sleeping at her grandparents'. I would start to pick fights with Tom, seeing things that sometimes weren't there. I remember one afternoon that I got up after working a night shift. Tom had got his mobile phone bill through and it was a stupid amount in the sum of five hundred and odd pounds. He was so good at telling me and he successfully convinced me that the network had made a massive mistake and that he would sort it out. No more was mentioned of it and I took it at face value.

Come late July, beginning of August, things went from bad to worse with my behavior. Some, though, for good reason, as one morning I came in from work and I needed to use Tom's phone to ring his mum, as the banns for the wedding were being read out in the church that morning and I was wondering if she was coming to church with us. Tom was in bed sound asleep as I brought his phone to life. It showed this message on his phone saying, "GOODNIGHT BABE XXX." I was in total shock. I quietly walked down the stairs without waking him up and rang his sister and told her about the message. Vanessa advised me to look through his phone to see if there were any more messages from that same number and that she would ring me back on my number in a few minutes. For the first time in our relationship I was one of those girls looking through her partners' phone. As I got up his message history there was text after text after text of this one number. As I opened and read them, I was so angry I didn't know what to do or where to turn. Then I started to open the picture messages she had sent of herself, proper sexy pictures and I just couldn't contain myself. She was stunning, long brown hair, very slim, and all I could see was this beautiful woman smiling back at me. In my head all I wanted to do was punch that fucking smile right off her face, how dare she! Vanessa rang me and I told her everything I had found, including the pictures of the woman.

Vanessa advised me to put the woman's phone number into my phone, don't do anything as yet and walk over to her mother's house as she was staying there. She told me to give the woman a call and get her side of the story first before confronting Tom. So I topped up my phone, opened a can of Stella to drink whilst I walked over to Tom's parents' house.

Oh boy, did the bitch tell me a lot. Tom had been carrying on with her since February, had actually told her he was a single parent as I walked out on him and our daughter. He was making plans to move my daughter and himself in with her, can you believe that he was making actual plans with this woman? Oh, and the best part was when Tom was away on his stag holiday in Magaluf, Spain, he was in contact with her throughout. Making out that the stag party he was on was actually his best mate's and he was the best man. I recall her telling me that she joked with Tom saying, "I bet it's your stag do, really" and that they laughed about it.

In response Tom told her, "No, not me, I'm never getting married."

Talk about being stunned, then suddenly I don't know what came over me. I lost it and shouted abuse down the phone at her and threatened her. Once I got to Tom's parents' house and told them everything and the conversation I had just had with the other woman, everyone was too shocked. His mother took the can of Stella off me, saying, "That isn't going to help the situation," and bloody poured it away down the flipping sink. Like "how bloody dare she" was all that was going off in my mind. Vanessa asked for the woman's phone number so she could ring her to talk, which of course I did and she went outside. Her parents got Vanessa's boyfriend to take them round to mine to see what was going on in Tom's head. They both were getting worried as the wedding was only a week away. I think they wanted to sort this sorry little mess out so the wedding would go ahead. His dad did ask me, though, before they went to mine, "Are you wanting to call the wedding off? We may still get some of the money back and we can start making phone calls to everyone."

I didn't know what I wanted, to be fair. My head was smashed with everything. I was tired and exhausted as I had finished my fourth night shift and not been to bed yet, had to make an excuse to the priest as to why we wouldn't be at church that morning for the banns to be read out; to put the topper on top of the cake (no pun intended) I had to now deal with the fact that my husband to be had been cheating on me for the last six months. I didn't know what I wanted to do; in my head I didn't want to let anyone down. All I wanted to do was go to bed and get some sleep, but that had to wait.

I had no idea what was going on at my place, but I guess it gave me time to think. Vanessa had come back indoors from her telephone conversation and calmly talked to me to understand the woman's point of view as she felt for her. Vanessa probably got more out of her then I did, to be fair. Apparently, they had met on a dating site. She thought she had found a nice single father and it went from there. If she had known he was engaged to be married, she would have told him where to go. She said that she was sorry for what had happened and promised that she had no idea about me; all she was told was that I had walked away from him and our little girl and never came back. How dare he use something from my past, the bastard, was all that was going on in my head.

After around half an hour Tom was here with his parents. They were talking outside and Vanessa's boyfriend Simon came in and told us both that as soon as his mum had got in the house she went straight upstairs into our bedroom and smacked Tom around the face whilst he was still in bed. He hadn't known what had hit him but was in total shock to see that it was his mother. Once he was inside the house, he sat down next to me and started to apologise and said that nothing had actually happened – it had always been over the phone, messages back and forth as well as some pictures. His parents had had our daughter overnight so they took her out and Vanessa and Simon went out with them, so me and Tom could have some time together to talk and decided what we wanted to do with regard to the wedding. In my head I didn't want to let anyone down, I didn't want people to look at me and feel pity, I didn't want to come across as a failure. In the back of my head I guess I also thought that if I get this man down the aisle and get married, everything would then be okay. There was also a lot of self-doubt going on around my head as if I was second guessing everything I was saying to Tom. It was as if I was forcing myself to believe everything Tom was telling me. I was wanting to believe it, living in a fantasy world wanting that happily ever after story. Then the question came. "So, what do you want to do about the wedding, do you still want to get married? Because I do." Then all the things I had done to Tom had started coming back to me, like one afternoon getting that drunk that Vanessa said I tried to kiss her boyfriend, which of course I do not remember at all. I do remember that Tom left me for a couple of days because of it. So because of that I had to forgive him too, even though in my head I was thinking to myself: hold on, that was a couple of weeks ago I did that; you have been carrying on for six months. Does one drunken mistake that I cannot remember cancel out his huge double life in a way that has carried on for months? I just didn't know anymore and further to that I didn't know what I wanted at that time, though I thought I loved this man and we had a child together – that must be worth saving. So the wedding would go ahead.

After the discussion I went to his mother's bedroom and

got on the bed to shut my eyes for a few minutes. Before I realised it, Tom came in, lay beside me, put his arms around me and I fell asleep. I didn't even hear his parents coming back in with my daughter. His mum had to come into the room to wake us up and as soon as we both got into the living room, we were asked, "Well then, what's going on? Is the wedding still going to go ahead as planned? Or would you rather postpone it till next year?"

My response was, "No, the wedding will go ahead as planned." That was that. No more mentioned, and it was buried under the carpet as though nothing had happened.

All the final preparations had been done and I had surprised Tom with a honeymoon, nowhere glamorous – I couldn't afford it. I managed to get us four days away to Prague. At least it was something; something is better than nothing, right? Who doesn't have some kind of a honeymoon when they get married?

Whilst I had all this going on, also at the end of July 2006 my stepfather turned up out of the blue at my house in Cumbria. Apparently, he told me he was concerned about me after talking to someone close to me at the time. Who explained to him that I wasn't in the best frame of mind and I was being physically abused again by an ex-partner. So after wearing that person down he managed to get my address from them and decided to just show up. I knew that he was married by then and I asked him how my children and his wife were. He didn't want to talk about his wife and he said that the children were doing fine. He always got it in there that the children didn't want to see me. So as I didn't want to drop the subject I asked him about the cards I had sent with the money and if the children had received them. His response was cruel and hurtful as he went on to tell me that he had destroyed the cards and letters I had sent as he didn't want me to have an involvement in their lives. I was in total shock and remember shouting at him to leave my house and it felt good to let it rip to his face, if truth be told, as that was the first real time I didn't hold back in fear of being scared of what he would do to me.

Afterwards, once he left, I wondered what to do for the best. He was destroying everything I was sending to the children. I bloody bet he kept the money for himself, though; that's what was going through my mind at the time. So in the end I did stop sending cards to the children. If they weren't receiving the cards, then they were not receiving the money I sent them. I feel as if this was yet another barrier put up by my stepfather and that he had blocked any and all contact I could have had with my children.

So here we were the day before the wedding. I had finished work now for two weeks to enjoy the wedding and the honeymoon, then a week at home to be with my new husband. There was still a lot to do. We dropped the wedding cake off at the venue, with the seating plan and the name of our song for our first dance as man and wife. If I recall correctly, I'm pretty sure the song was by the 80s group Madness – *It Must Be Love*. That was Tom's choice as he wasn't into proper romantic cheesy music like me. Once that was done, we had to then get to the church for our wedding rehearsal with all the wedding party. There was one part in the rehearsal when the priest says to us, "If anyone thinks why this couple shouldn't get married, then please hold up your hand." Guess what I go and do and everyone actually laughed? I was the one that put her hand up. Everyone that was there thought I was joking. Then when it came to the end of the practice where you are supposed to walk out together, I just walked away from Tom and took back up the aisle on my own. His sister made a jokey comment about it.

What they didn't know was that I was having this inner turmoil with myself. So many doubts, fears and questions that I had no answers to. I was questioning myself: do I really want to marry this man? But I am 24, I don't want to be left on the shelf. I can't easily walk away if he cheats on me. Can I really trust him? Can I really see myself being with him for the rest of my life through the good times and the bad? The answer was NO. All the hurt and pain and then all the flashbacks were rushing at me; the pain and trauma that I had been through with my stepfather came back to haunt me. So what do I go and do that night? I score a gram of cocaine, go back to my sister-in-law to be as I am staying at hers for the night with a couple of bottles of wine. I get drunk and high as a kite until I am off my head and finally, I escape all my fears and troubles, thinking that Tom will hurt me again, maybe not now but he will for sure in the future.

As I finally try and settle and go to sleep, me and Vanessa hear her front door being unlocked and there suddenly is her boyfriend Simon and her eighteen-year-old son, Jake. Talk about being surprised. "Why aren't you with Tom?" Me and Vanessa ask in unison. Apparently, the groom's party went back to our place with a few more drinks. However, Simon and Jake wanted to get some food so came back home to get something to eat. Suddenly Simon was getting all kissy kissy with Vanessa, so I got up and went downstairs to talk to Jake.

This is the part where the night takes a bad turn, me and Jake were messing about in the kitchen and Jake goes to pick me up but as he had a few drinks too many, he accidentally drops me right on my back and it hurt my spine badly and winded me in the process. We were laughing about it, and he kindly carried me in to the living room and laid me on the sofa and sat on the floor next to me apologizing. I told him not to be silly, I was okay. Somehow, we got onto the subject of Tom and having that telephone relationship and how it carried on for six months. He went on further, saying that Tom had actually used Jake's phone to send her a couple of messages as he had run out of credit. I was in shock. It was as if he wanted to be caught out. Was Tom having doubts as well? Had he done that knowing if his sister had found out she would tell me and I would cancel the whole wedding? Then, somehow, I don't know how it happened, but we both moved in to kiss each other. We must have only been kissing a few seconds when Vanessa pulls Jake into the kitchen and starts hitting him. Shit, we had been caught. Straight away I got dressed and told Vanessa I was walking back to mine and I would tell Tom about the kiss; it was the least I could do.

Whilst walking back to mine I had twenty minutes to think of what I was going to say to him. Nothing in my head made any sense, though. As the fresh air was hitting me the drink was sending me dizzy as well as the drugs I had. I still had a bit left, so I quickly took it whilst walking. No-one would notice what I was doing. I just pretended I was giving my nose a wipe. By the time I got to the front door I was pretty shit faced but also confident.

Tom was surprised to see me. I just said to him, "Look, can we talk upstairs, in private?" as I didn't want to tell him in front of his mates. So upstairs we go and with every step I am taking I am getting more and more nervous. A huge ball of knots was squeezing my stomach so tightly I couldn't breathe.

I was panicking and my nerves were standing on end. Once in the bedroom we sat on the bottom of the bed and I just told him the truth of what happened. I may have put the blame on Jake, to be fair. I think I made out he made the first move, when in fact it was both of us together. Straight away Tom said, "Well, don't think we are getting married in the morning."

My only response was, "Can you not forgive me? I forgave you, and that went on for six months." The difference was she was a stranger, whereas Jake was a family member, Tom's nephew.

Vanessa, Jake and Simon had all arrived at mine whilst me and Tom had both been upstairs, and she couldn't wait to tell the lads about what was going on. Things got out of control quite rapidly, arguments broke out, I started screaming and shouting at the top of my voice, screaming at everyone to get the fuck out of my house, then something came over me. I cannot explain it but I went into our downstairs bathroom, got some of the broken glass from the window, went to the living room window, held my left arm out and cut my arm from my wrist to my elbow. I had cut right through the skin and all my muscle. I then collapsed onto the living room floor. I had a complete breakdown; my life as I knew it had snowballed downhill vastly. All the trauma, all the abuse, everything came to a head and I tried to end it there and then.

As I lay there on my living room floor, all I could remember was the front door opening and in walked Tom, Vanessa and someone else; I don't know who, to be fair. One of Tom's mates was shouting out, "Quick, quick, phone for an ambulance, she is losing a lot of blood."

The next thing I recall is Vanessa being above me calling me a stupid cow and, "You've only done this for the attention," and accused me of being like her sister. All she was doing was throwing insult after insult at me. Then I passed out. I came around again. I was in hospital and my arm was stinging and I was crying out in pain. I had been set up to an IV drip; they were trying to flush the drink and drugs out of my system, I guess, and also, I was being giving morphine for the pain. I had to have emergency surgery later on that morning.

I was in surgery for quite a few hours. I needed to have lots of internal stitches, and externally I needed my skin to be stitched, stapled and glued back together. In total I had seventy stitches and staples. It was a good job that my arm was completely numb when it came for them to be taken out two or three weeks later. I was kept in hospital for around five days and had visits from the mental health nurses and finally was released from the hospital. I only had the one visit from Tom; that was to give me back my house keys as he was moving out, as the relationship was over and to inform me that I wasn't going to have my daughter he was keeping, and the only way I could see her is if he was there to supervise the visit. He thought I was unsafe to be around her and mentally not fit to be a mother. I wasn't going to go through that again and lose another child, so whilst in the hospital I rang the solicitors, told them everything that had happened, was honest and open, right down to what I had done to myself and that I was in the hospital at that moment. An appointment was made for when I was to be let out.

Chapter 10

Once I was back home, I actually hated the place. In the short twelve months I had lived there it was starting to have bad memories. There was still dried blood from my accident there on my wooden floor; the suitcase that was packed for what was supposed to be my honeymoon was in the corner. The bathroom was a mess, broken glass in the sink. The whole house was just a depressing dark hole that I wanted to escape. At the weekend I went out with my next-door neighbor and one of her friends. She thought she would take me into town and have a night out. It had been a tough couple of days with appointments here and there. So I thought, okay then, I will go out and let my hair down and forgot about my problems for a few hours. After a couple of hours, we thought we would go to another pub to have a dance and that, as I love to dance. As soon as we get in there and go to the bar for drinks, who do I run into but Vanessa coming out of the women's toilets. As I follow her to see where she goes, who else is there but Tom and his mates all hammered in the corner of the pub? So the best thing to do was to leave and go elsewhere.

There was a problem with this, though. Now that Vanessa knew I was out, every place I went into she and her boyfriend would follow us. So in the end it came to a point where I wasn't able to enjoy myself anymore and I took a taxi back home, not before, though, she saw me and my neighbor's brother kissing each other. Stupid? Yes. Worth it? I don't know.

It wasn't long after this, it was the following week that Tom got the letter from my solicitors saying I was going to go to court as I wanted my child to live with me. He started to let me see her more regularly and coming round for tea or a takeaway. I started to feel good about it. Then a week later on a Sunday morning I received a phone call from his mother asking if Tom had stayed over at mine, and was he still there? "No, he isn't here. Why?" His mother went on to tell me that he had gone out the previous day and had not come back and no one could get him on his mobile. They were struggling a little with my daughter, so straight away I got ready and walked to theirs. I was there within twenty minutes. I got all her things together, packed them up, as Vanessa came through the front door. She was nice to me and said she would give us both a lift back to mine. As we were leaving Tom was just getting in and you could tell he had been on a session. I didn't look back. I got my daughter and I just got out of there.

As time went on, I did allow Tom to see his daughter. He would come and pay visits and spend time with the two of us. One evening before he went after I put my daughter to bed, we ended up kissing before he left to go back to his sister's. Around ten minutes later he rings me from a phone box and asks me to get back together with him. To be fair, I still loved the bloke, so straight away I said, "Yes, okay then." When he came back the following morning with his stuff, we sat on the sofa and had a long talk about things and said that we would put it all behind us so long as nothing like this ever happened again.

It was all going okay as well. We tried for another baby and were successful within the first month of trying and everyone was overjoyed for the two of us. Me and Tom were both happy with the good news. Then something happened. I don't know what it was. I just had a feeling, so I went through his phone and there was this woman's home number and mobile number in his phone and I sent her a text and she confirmed that she worked at the factory with him and they had got close. That was it for me; we had only been back together for two months and Tom was at it again. I got his stuff and threw him out there and then.

I had a good cry about the situation. I was four weeks pregnant and just got a new job. Again, I felt all alone, no-one to turn to, none to help with my daughter when I would go to work. Then, to add insult to injury, Tom came round one evening to see his daughter and to put her to bed. Afterwards he wanted to talk about the pregnancy. He wanted me to consider having a termination, as I would find it hard to bring two kids up under the age of two, plus start a new job. He was laying it on pretty thick, whilst I was sitting there crying my eyes out. I had no one to talk to. I was really and truly on my own.

I had some big decisions to make, and there was only me that could make them; no one could make them for me. Firstly, no one was forcing me into getting rid of my baby. It was the easiest decision to make; I was keeping it no matter what. The second decision was a little bit harder; what was I going to do about my new job? After a couple of days thinking about it, I rang the company and explained my position and thanked them for the job but at this moment in time I couldn't take it. I had to put my daughter and unborn child first. They were understanding and wished me well for the future and hoped all goes well.

Following Christmas 2006 I learned that Tom had found himself a new girlfriend via the internet on some dating site. It upset me, I'm not going to lie. I think I might have been a bit of a bitch about it, to be fair. I knew that they hadn't met each other face to face as yet, but it was coming. In January after my second scan, which Tom came to, we discovered that we were having a son, and to be fair, he was excited as now he had one of each. In the back of my head I was wondering if he would resemble my two older children. I kind of hoped he would, just a little bit.

Following this I had the shock of my life around two or three weeks later when I discovered that Tom wanted to do a DNA test on our son as now, he didn't believe that he was the father. Something that his sister had told him, apparently. Well, if that was the case, I would have the last laugh when he spends all that money just for the test to prove that he was the father, the stupid idiot always listening to what others are having to say, not having his own mind. I was starting to realise how much better off without him I really was. I was at the stage now that one minute I loved him and then with the next breath I bloody hated him with a passion. For the first time in my life I truly understood the meaning behind the saying "there's a thin line between love and hate", and boy, was that true!

My pregnancy was quite tough throughout. I was in and out of hospital on a few occasions as my pelvis had dropped a bit. Labor wasn't much better; it was the hardest of all four of my births. My labor pains started on a Sunday night as I was only in the early stages and progression was moving slowly. I was sent home. I was back in Monday afternoon and that was me in hospital until after my son was born. He wasn't born until Thursday afternoon, talk about being lazy and not wanting to move or make an appearance, which is the same today, to be honest. The longest labor out of all four births and the most traumatic, but worth every single second.

I couldn't wait to get home and be alone with both my children. I knew I was on my own and I knew it wasn't going to be an easy ride but I was looking forward to it nonetheless. Tom and Vanessa came to pick me and my new-born son up from the hospital and took us both home. Once I was home and settled Tom and Vanessa both left me to it and about an hour later his mother and father came round and paid me a visit to see us both and to drop off my daughter and after a hour or so they too left me to it. I was nervous being left on my own, if truth be told, but do you know what? I managed perfectly well on my own. I got into a really good routine with both the children and with myself, all three of us with both bedtime routine and waking up. I started to get out more and went to the mother and baby groups and started to get my own circle of friends. I was finally starting to get a life of my own.

After my boy turned three months old, I started to look for a job part time and nurseries for the children. It only took me a couple weeks to find a job that suited the working hours that I wanted and fitted in with the times and days I could put my children into nursery. It was here that my friendship circle got bigger and I became close friends with one girl called Becky. We just hit it off and we have been good friends ever since. The girls from work would try to get me out on many occasions at the weekends, for which I always made excuses not to go, because I didn't want to ask anyone if they could look after my children. Until one weekend when Tom wanted to have the children for the weekend down at his fiancée's house with him, so I agreed and I made plans to go out with

Becky and a couple of the other girls from work. I had a fantastic weekend and it felt good to let my hair down and have some fun. In a way I had the best of both worlds. Be a good full-time mother and then every other weekend when Tom and his fiancée had the children for the weekend, I could have my time and go out without feeling guilty.

It was the last bank holiday in May 2008 and whilst at work the girls were planning a night out and were begging me to go out with them. Becky kept going on about this lad that she wanted to set me up with. Telling me how good looking he was and that he was a really lovely lad and that we would get on, just give him a chance. In response I remember saying to her, "Becky, look, I'm not interested in meeting anyone, I don't need fixing up." Becky wouldn't give up, though, so half an hour before our shift finished, she had managed to convince me to go out and meet this lad on a blind date, promising me, though, that she will be there all the time. After work we went into town for a quick drink as we always finished early on a Friday. Once we had a drink, I had to leave her to pick up my children and get them to their grandparents' house for Tom to pick them up. Then I went back to mine to get my things together as I was spending the night at Becky's and waited for the taxi to pick me up.

Once at Becky's she poured me a large glass of wine and informed me that my mysterious blind date was up for meeting me that night. I started to get butterflies and excited. She got me to get into the shower and get ready. Once she had done her hair and makeup she started on my hair and I did my own makeup. I remember I had a cute pink checked shirt on with a little ruffle skirt and wedge shoes. I looked pretty good, if truth be told. There was one thing, though; I had buttoned my shirt right up, and Becky laughed at me and undid a couple of my buttons and said to me, "Get those babies on show, you have a good rack, you should show them off more." To be fair, I did have great boobs.

Well, here we were hitting the town and as eight o'clock came me and Becky went to the pub where we were meeting my blind date and his mate. I remember being that nervous I couldn't have my usual drink and wanted to keep a clear head so I wouldn't make a drunken mistake, so I was drinking coke whilst Becky was having her usual pints of Fosters. I had to go to the toilet so close to meeting my blind date but I couldn't wait any longer. As I was returning back to Becky outside in the front beer garden, I walked past a lad that caught my eye. He was quite tall, dressed in jeans, white shirt and a pink tie that was hanging loosely around his neck; he was so good looking that after I walked past him I looked back over my shoulder to take another look, and as I did he was looking back at me and we just smiled, and that was it.

Once I was back outside, I had to tell Becky that I had just seen a really good-looking lad. I actually made a joke and said to her, "If I don't like this lad you have set me up with, I will try and look for that hottie." We were laughing as I looked over to the door and who do I see but the hot guy. He was with his mate and they were both coming over to where we were standing having a smoke.

Then the hottie spoke, "All right, Becs, how you doing?"

Then Becky turned around to me and introduced us both, "Lily, this is Aaron, Aaron, this is Lily." The hottie was my blind date. I couldn't believe it. Wow! Becky may have just got it right, but in the back of my head the sensible part was telling me that looks aren't everything. Also, I had slight panic setting in because I had always said to myself that I wouldn't get involved with anyone because I had a daughter to protect as well as my son, but more so my little girl. As I didn't want history to repeat itself, no way was my little girl going to go through what I did with my stepfather. I guess I was making out in my head that because my father was like that, then all men would be. I know that it was a stupid way of thinking, that not all men were sick and twisted, but once you have been through the crap that I had, it kind of leaves a few scars.

We did have a great night, though. Aaron was a nice bloke and we got on really well, even shared a few kisses throughout the night. We all went back to Becky's where we all slept over and the next morning the three of us went to McDonalds for breakfast. Then me and Becky said goodbye to Aaron, and that was that. Until two days later whilst I was at the park with the kids when Becky texted me to ask if she could give Aaron my phone number as he had been at her all weekend for it. At first, I told her no; I explained that the kids came first and I had no time for a relationship and I told myself that I didn't actually like Aaron and he wasn't for me. So I thought that was that and I wouldn't hear anything about him again.

Then around a week and a half later I went to the cinema to watch the first *Sex and the City* movie with a couple of girlfriends and afterwards we went to the pub for a drink before going home. As we were walking up the street to the pub, who do we bump into? No one other than Becky and her mate Nicole, and they were with Aaron and his group of mates and, as it appeared, we were all going to the same pub. However, me and my two mates decided to sit separately from them, apart from Becky and Nicole who decided to also sit with us. It was a nice way to finish my evening as I had to get back home to my children. Half an hour before I went but who comes over? None other than Aaron. I recall him casually walking over, pulling a chair out and he just sat there and joined in the conversation, making everyone laugh and putting me at ease. Again, he was lovely, so chilled and laid back; as it came for me to say my goodbyes to leave and get back home Aaron just sat there, smiled up at me and said goodbye, so I just gave him a hug and a kiss on the cheek and said goodbye.

I wasn't going to admit it to anyone but when I saw Aaron, I actually got butterflies in my stomach and I got that silly little nervous feeling. You know, as you do when you are a teenager, well, that was the way I was feeling. On the outside, however, I was playing it cool and maybe a little stand-offish, as if we were plain and simply mates and nothing else. Which made it a little surprising that the following day Aaron had stayed over at Becky's and I came up in conversation and he was bugging her for my mobile number once again. So to get him off Becky's back I agreed for her to pass on my number. He didn't bloody waste any time either. Aaron texted me about ten minutes afterwards, talk about being keen, and in a way for me it was a little bit of a put-off, but I wasn't going to be rude. I texted him back and told him I'll get in touch later as I was out with my children. I didn't put any kisses on the end of the text as he had. If I remember rightly, he had put three on the end of his message. I think he got the message as when he replied there wasn't a kiss at the end, and that made me laugh.

We spent the next week or two casually sending a text here and there, never arranging to meet up as I wasn't really ready for that. Then he was going away with his dad for a week. Whilst he was away I had to go into hospital for an operation, in which unfortunately something went seriously wrong as I ended up with bad internal bleeding that went unnoticed for hours, even though my blood pressure was dropping all the time and I couldn't get up because I would always feel faint. I had to have emergency surgery, where I had to be fully cut open and the internal bleeding had to be drained out. I was really poorly; a simple op as a day patient turned into a nightmare from hell that I nearly died from. I ended up in hospital for over a week, three blood transfusions and a bad throat and feeling weak. There was one good thing that came out of it, though.

As soon as Aaron got back home from his holiday, Becky let him know I was in hospital as I had gone through a bad time of it. He had only really known me a couple of weeks. He came to visit me a couple of times and it was that that made me look at him in a different light. What bloke after only knowing a woman for a couple of weeks would do the three-mile walk to pay a visit to someone they had just met and were getting to know? Well, I'll tell you, not many, very, very few. So that was the start of the relationship and it just got stronger and stronger from there. After two weeks whilst me, Becky, Aaron and Finn, Becky's then boyfriend were on a double date, me and Aaron thought we would go elsewhere on our own and whilst we were in this bar we were talking about things we both wanted for the future and Aaron turned around to me and said, "What would you say if I asked you to marry me?"

I went all giggly and was surprised, but it was my response that surprised me more as I said, "Are you asking me to marry you? If you are, I would say yes."

The next day Aaron and me went out and he bought me my engagement ring. Nearly six and a half months later me and Aaron were married in the December of 2008.

Now don't get me wrong; it was good, but we had a lot of ups and downs heading our way. Firstly, I had to start talking a bit about my past. I had already told him about my two older children and that their father had been my father, which had to go on to the next conversation which I just skirted around, never went into much details as I never really wanted to talk about it. After I had been drinking on a night out or had a girls' day out and I would arrive home absolutely drunk I would end up having an argument with Aaron over the stupidest of things. He may have said something to me, and I would take it in the wrong context and I would put my barriers up and become defensive and argumentative. It was as if I was pushing him away, I didn't want to let him in and get too close. How at times it didn't end our marriage with my behavior I don't know because I really was a nasty bitch at times. I guess I was seeing how far I could push him, if that makes any sense. It was as if I was trying to prove to myself that he too was like other guys. You know something, though, he actually proved me wrong and also, he proved to me that there are also good guys out there that still exist. So slowly and surely, bit by bit, those bricks would slowly come down and I would let him in a little bit at a time, and as time went on, I trusted him enough to talk about my past and what I had been through.

Aaron never once judged me or made me to feel bad at all. Instead, at times when I would allow him too, he would simply come up to me, put his arms around my body and just hold me without saying any words. Other times I would cry on his shoulder whilst he would talk calmly and soothingly to me. Don't get me wrong, there were times, especially through the hard things that any person would struggle to deal with that would really anger him, and he wanted to deal with the situation himself. He just simply wanted to protect me and do what it took to make me feel safe. He would always sit there on the sofa and listen to me talk about my children that were born to my stepfather. He would support me when it came to me trying to give them a ring to talk to them, but my stepfather wouldn't allow it; he would always find a way to stop it. So he encouraged me to write to them, which I was already doing. I never missed a birthday or Christmas. It was nice to have someone beside me that supported me and was there through it all, the good and the bad. As time went on Aaron would sometimes bring my past up and told me that maybe it was time that I went to the police, but time and time again I would always give the same answer, "No, just let it go, I have moved on now and I haven't got the strength to go through that. It would be like opening an old can of worms. Just leave it." There wasn't a day that didn't go by that I didn't think of the two children, wondering what they were into, what they both looked like, how they were getting on in life, did they ever think about me, most of all what had they been told about me and why I left.

Looking back on it now, I guess I gave my father the perfect situation to wipe my existence out of the family completely. As there would be no difficult questions being asked, nothing had to be explained, like: why were my siblings the children's siblings? Will my siblings be their siblings or aunties and uncles? Would my mother be known as grandmother or as something else? How would that go down, so yes, in a way, me going as I did, made everything a lot more simple for my dad to explain, and the family dynamic, I guess, wouldn't now have been questioned. Oh, I don't know, I could be wrong, but that is my thinking or opinion.

Chapter 11

In 2014 something horrible happened to both my younger children which was too close to home. Things that they had been suffering through family members of my ex-partner that I had no idea about whatsoever. One morning it was my little boy who spoke up, and it wasn't to me, it was to Aaron, my husband who both my children now called Dad. Then when we spoke to my daughter about what was being said and what had come to light and she went on to tell us her version of events, then I had to do something. I wasn't going to allow history to repeat itself. There was me thinking about not getting involved with another man because I had a daughter and I didn't want to happen to her what had happened to me. When all along I should have been worried about the biological side of their father's family instead. As I don't want to go into it, all I will say on this matter is after my children had been talked to on many occasions and interviewed all contact with that side of the family was stopped.

The following months were really hard for the children; they both had to receive counselling and attend therapy sessions. My daughter couldn't go into town because of fear and anxiety of maybe bumping into them. So we thought the best thing for us as a family was to move a couple of towns away from Carlisle towards the West of Cumbria and into the Lake District. Whilst the children were attending counselling,

I also took the opportunity of taking a few sessions myself and seeing if I was actually ready to deal with my own personal issues that ran deep into my own past. If I didn't do it now, then I would never do it. I had to be a lot stronger for my younger children as they needed me to be there one hundred percent for them, not doing a half-hearted job because I got too emotional and too involved because of my own past. So yes, it was time for me to face up to the abuse I had suffered from the physical to the emotional to the mental, leading all the way to being raped.

As the sessions went on, I think it was towards the end of 2014 in the December, I recall sitting in my living room with my husband Aaron once we had put the children to bed and I said to him, "If I can do it for my kids, especially my daughter, then I need to show them that I can also do it for myself. I need to take a stand and I need to do this for myself." Aaron simply came closer to me, hugged me and said that he was with me all the way.

You see all that time I was also trying to protect my mother as I also witnessed all the bad shit that my father had done to her all throughout my life and she did have to put up with a lot. However, the difference is when my child needed me to protect them, I did it without any guilt or doubt or at the risk of falling outs, I made sure I did what I needed to protect my children. That is what makes me different to her, I guess, and that was the turning point in my thinking towards her.

Everything seemed to come together in my thought pattern, especially once I was placed in a situation a little similar to my own. As a mother you want to protect your children and you will do everything and anything to do that. Instead my mother did no such thing when it got so tough for her that she couldn't handle the situation. Then, in a way, I was her pawn. In my opinion she was just as bad, if not worse, than my father as she knew it was going on, she allowed it to go on and worst of all she too was involved in the abuse as she would stand there outside the bedroom door once she woke me up, got me into her and his bedroom door, she would close the door behind me and wait on the landing until I came out. Of course, she would have heard me say no to him and she would have heard the cries coming from me, but never once did she try to help.

So once I was facing something similar with my own children, it showed how different I truly was to her. So I was no longer worried about her or trying to protect her from the police, as she too had to face up to what her part was for the abuse I faced from both my parents. So once I had made my mind up and spoke to Aaron about it, I rang up the police in Lancashire at the start of January 2015 and explained everything to them and reported the abuse I suffered. After speaking to the police officer and he had finished taking notes, it was explained to me that someone more senior will be in contact with me and they will take it from there. Once I was off the phone, I was a shaky mess. That first step had been taken. I guess the hard bit was to come.

It was a couple of days later that a more senior police officer rang me up, where I had to go into a bit more detail and explain things at a greater length and I remember thinking to myself, can I really do this? Here I am, literally going to turn a lot of people's lives upside-down, can I really do that? I was always questioning and at times second guessing myself. Then I would look at my children and the other thoughts would replace the negative ones such as: if I can do it for my children, then why can't I do it for myself? How am I ever going to move on and leave the past behind me if I don't face it? I had a really good support network around me too. So I carried on forward and once me and the police officer had finished on the phone, he went on to explain that a video interview would have to be done, and could I go back to my home town to do this? As much as this put a knot in my stomach, I agreed to do it. So a date was set for me to do my official police interview for March of 2015.

I was worried about my mental health, so I booked an appointment with my doctor a few days later. Once I was in that doctor's office and I started to tell her what was going on and what I was going to be doing I just broke down crying. It was as if a dam had burst, it was as if finally, all these suppressed emotions I had locked away and ignored over the years were edging to the surface and I didn't know how to control it anymore. The doctor must have seen the distress in me because straight away I was put back onto anti-depressants and referred to the Mental Health Services. I wasn't regretting my decision about going to the police but I was worried about being put on the spot, going to court and being asked hard and at times difficult questions. Most importantly, having my words listened to and being believed after such a long time, because it wasn't as if it had just happened; eleven years had now passed by. If it went to court, it was getting twelve strangers of the jury to believe me and listen to my voice. On the other side I was opening up a can of worms. What clever, dirty tricks would both my parents play? So a lot of things were swimming around in my head.

I heard from the Mental Health Services pretty much straight away, and this time I never ran away. I actually stuck to it, even though at times I found it incredibly difficult. For the first time ever, I was wanting to face things head on and not hide away anymore. I had to answer a lot of questions and I had to be completely honest about my feelings and emotions and be up front about my past. I had to fill in forms and questionnaires so the doctors could make a proper diagnosis, if there was any to make, with regard to mental health disorders. After around two weeks of talking and going to a couple of sessions and once all the paperwork had been filled in, I was diagnosed with Depression, Complex PTSD and Emotional Unstable Personality Disorder. So I was put onto a few medications to keep me in a way under control because my personality was changing. I was getting more and more angry, losing my temper, lashing out.

Unable to sleep amongst many other issues that were suddenly appearing.

Finally, the day had arrived where I had to get the train back to Lancashire and to my home town, where I was to be picked up by the police officer who was in charge of my case, and he would take me to the offices where my police video interview was to take place. I tell you something; that had to be one of the worst things that I have ever had to do at that moment in my life. It was all sweetness and light to start off with; then I had to go into detail starting from the very beginning. The problem was, though, that it wasn't just telling the police about what had happened, but I had to go into the facts of everything and into the tiniest of details. It was so hard, and it made me feel so sick to my stomach, especially having to talk about the sexual abuse and the rape. As I had to give actual details of where I was touched, what touched what, was it on the outside of clothing or inside the clothing, skin on skin.

Talking about it was getting cruder and cruder, as it had to be on record, every tiny detail where no stone was left unturned. It was so difficult and hard, but I also understood why the police wanted me to go into so much detail. I think the interview lasted for around three hours, maybe a little bit more. Once it was over, I simply couldn't wait to get back onto the train and get as far away from there as possible and run home to where I felt safe and lock myself away from everyone and everything.

I started to become a recluse and wouldn't want to go out anywhere. I was starting to shut the outside world out, I didn't feel safe to be out in public. If anyone said anything to me, I would take it in the wrong way and lash out or face up to people, and that included young teenagers. I was losing myself and who I was, and I couldn't control it. I was changing as a person. It was as if a darkness had escaped from me and was trying to keep me under its control, I was losing an inner battle with myself and I let the darkness grab onto me. I felt so alone, even though I had so many people around. I had learned to put on a front so people couldn't see the turmoil I was actually suffering inside. The only people who knew what I was suffering mentally and physically were my husband and, at times, my children. To release my anger and frustrations I would self-harm quite badly or drink too much. It was my way to relieve all my pressure to let go of the pain. No matter how many times people say it will be okay or a little better in the end or, "I can try to understand what it must have been like", in my head I was like… how can you even say that? No one will ever know what it was like to live through that kind of shit and suffer in such an inhumane way, unless you have been through it yourself. So to keep me on a level mood I had to take my medications and attend all my sessions. The problem was I knew it was going to get a lot more difficult and tougher before it would start to get a little bit better and easier.

In July 2015, after a long few months, of the police getting together as much evidence as they could possibly find, both my parents were arrested. That was a really long day. I only knew of the day that the arrest would happen and from there I was in the dark. I was stressing out so much thinking all kinds of things. The worst that could happen was both my parents being let go. As my father had always had the gift of the gab and could always do his best to talk his way out of situations, as he had done many times through my life. Nine times out of ten he would always get away with things without any repercussions and getting off scot free. So in my head I was thinking that it would happen again and he would walk away from this, and if so, he would come after me for going to the police.

Then that put into my mind a different kind of fear and that was the fear for my family. So yes, it was a really long day and my husband kept saying to me that no news is good news. The arrest happened around eight in the morning, I think, and finally at just gone eleven that same night I heard from the leading officer, who informed me that both my parents had been charged and were going to appear in front of the judge the following day and that they were going to ask the judge for my father to be kept in on remand until the hearing. At last I managed to breathe a small sigh of relief; now the hard bit was going to happen.

There were going to be two different trials. One was going to be through a family court and one was going to be the criminal court hearing. I found out that the first court appearance was going to be at the family courts. There had to be a few appearances before a judge before the case could begin. It was August of 2015 and I had to make an appearance and for the first time I would have to face both my parents. It was just a formality and I remember shitting myself, I was feeling sick with nerves and the anxiety that was building up was unreal. Luckily enough I was able to have my husband come into the courtroom with me whilst we sat there listening to both judges, one that was going to be overseeing the family hearing and one that was overseeing the criminal hearing.

My father was sat at the back behind a glass screen. I can still remember the sound of the chains rattling when the guards brought him up. My mother, as she wasn't on remand but still had to attend all the hearings, walked into the court room and walked past me and my husband and we looked at each other and there was nothing there; it was as if she was dead behind the eyes, no remorse, no sadness, no nothing. My mother was taken to sit in the back where my father had been placed behind the screen.

The hearing began and within around ten minutes I started to hear little whimpers and they were getting louder and louder. They were coming from my mother; she was becoming hysterical to a point where the judge that was talking had to stop the proceedings of the court. The reason why she was so hysterical was because she was put in the back like a caged criminal and was having to sit next to my stepfather. So the judge had to allow her to come from behind the screening area and sit on the back row of the court. Where suddenly she had stopped crying. In my head I was thinking, is she for real? Is she putting on an act? I couldn't believe it, but at the same time she was managing to make me feel guilty. I actually thought to myself, "Crap, should I be doing this to her as she had already suffered so much at the hands of my father?" Then my own daughter came into my thoughts and my young boy and what they had recently had gone through and soon I was thinking, "No, she was a mother who failed me, who had a hand in everything that had happened. I have no reason to feel ashamed or guilty."

The hearing lasted around thirty minutes or thereabouts and I couldn't wait to be out of there and get as far away from them as possible. An old friend of mine came to pick me up and straight away I asked to be taken to the shop for a bottle of wine. Instead of getting one I got two bottles. I wanted to drink to forget and be happier, I wanted to escape instead of facing up to how I was really feeling, because you have to remember I hadn't seen either one of my parents for eleven years. Then, bang! Seeing them both in this kind of situation was not the best; I had a whole lot of memories rushing back, fears, feeling scared, it was as if I had gone back in time and once again, I was fearful. Instead of discussing my feelings and emotions I buried them down deeply, got drunk and made an appearance that I was all okay; it was something I was becoming so good at now.

Later that day, however, everything came crashing down around me. All I can remember is that I managed to get the train home with my husband and children. As we got off the train and started walking back to our house, I felt myself go into an epileptic seizure. As I fell towards the ground, my head took a big part of the impact; that was it. I woke up in hospital not knowing my husband or children. I thought that the doctors and nurses were part of my parents' circle and they were going to abuse me. I recall me screaming and shouting for them to get away from me, thinking that they were there to rape me. Apparently, I had lost my current memory and had gone back in time and to me, I was fourteen again and I was reliving the abuse. I had a full mental breakdown and I had to be put under a section two and taken to a specialized hospital where I would have to stay under this section for up to twenty-eight days. If I tried to leave, then the police would have had to be called and would have to pick me up for my own protection.

My memory started coming back gradually and I remembered my husband and children after a few days and after nearly two weeks I was released from the hospital and allowed back home. To be fair, though, I didn't want to leave the safety of the hospital, I didn't want to go home. If I could have, I would have stayed in there for as long as I possibly could. My memory was still a little fuzzy, which worried me, and some of my memory still hasn't come back to this day. The next step for the mental health professionals was getting me mentally fit to face the court trials. I know that letters had been written to the senior officer in charge of my case to inform them of what had happened and that it was in my best interest for me to give my evidence via a video link. To be fair, this was put into place for both trials, which released a huge amount of strain from my shoulders, because if truth be told, if I had to testify in the same courtroom as them, then I would have bottled it. I thought I was strong enough, I thought I could do it without it bothering me or having an effect on me; obviously, I was wrong. I actually thought to myself that with all the time that had passed and building myself up and becoming a strong independent woman I could tackle this and get through it unscathed, but it had the opposite effect on me. It took me right back to my youth and to the worst parts of my life where I was always living in fear and pain.

Things changed a lot for me with regard to my home life. I couldn't have my husband touch me without flinching. It actually came to a point where my husband was even scared to come too close to me, especially after what had happened after my nervous breakdown, as I thought that he was my stepfather and I was apparently shouting rape when my husband came close to me. So yes, my relationship with him took a massive step backwards. It was as if we were friends that lived together. As for my job that I loved, they had to let me go as I was having too much time off and with me being sectioned and having a nervous breakdown, they knew that I wasn't in the right head space to carry out my duties and be professional. I was working as a Nursing Assistant at the time on the Emergency Admissions Unit, so we would have had all walks of life coming onto the ward for all kinds of treatments. So I understood why they had to let me go, but to be fair, my ward sister always said that I could go back once I had dealt with everything and got the right help for myself.

Slowly I was losing what I had made of my life. Things were changing and I didn't like it. I was sinking deeper and deeper into darkness and I was self-harming more and more. It was the only way that I could release the tension and anger that I was feeling. At the time when I was harming myself through cutting, I actually found it pleasing; weird, isn't it how something that is causing you pain can also be pleasing at the same time? I needed to get myself in the right head space and concentrate on getting through the court cases and dealing with some heavy-handed questions, as I knew what my parents' defence would be setting out to try and prove that I was lying and making it all up.

Chapter 12

Well here we were, November 2015 and the start of the family trial. Oh, that feeling I was going through. A mixture of dizziness, sickness, anxiety and the feeling to run away and don't turn back. I put on a good front, though, and walked into my nearest courts with my husband with my head held high, remembering with every step that I took that it was me that was the innocent party, me that had suffered at the hands of these people, I have no reason to feel or be ashamed. As long as I went in there and told the truth with every question that got thrown at me and stuck to the truth, then I would have done all the best that I could possibly do. The rest of it was in the judge's hands. There wouldn't be a jury, as it was in the family courts as there were still young children to be taken into account. So I felt a huge amount of pressure that was being put onto my shoulders. I also remember thinking to myself: what are the chances of me being believed by the judge and actually have my words really listened to? Well, I couldn't turn back now. I had come this far; it won't be long before it was over. It came to a point where I just wanted to get it over and done with.

I found it so much easier than I thought it would be, and the reason for that was because I was in a different city and giving my evidence via a video link. I couldn't thank everyone involved for setting this up and helping to make it easier for me.

The first day of questioning began and to start off with, I had in a way shut myself down, I was cold and withdrawn. It was as if I was there in person, a small shell of myself, but the voice that was talking was cold and blunt, as if it belonged to someone else. As time went on, though, and the questions were getting harder and I had to go into more detail, that barrier or walls that I had tried to keep around me for protection was slowly slipping away and my vulnerable side that I was doing my best not to allow out was starting to show. I didn't want my parents to witness that it was getting to me because in my head, by allowing that vulnerable side to show it was as if they were still winning, they would know that I was still scared and afraid of them. My brain wasn't processing that, actually. I wasn't being weak, but actually I was taking a stand and being strong and brave.

The questioning continued for two and a half days. I had never been so drained mentally or physically; it took so much out of me and also it took a bit from me as well. My father's solicitors were the worst of all the solicitors. His defence was going along the lines that it was me that came on to him and it was me doing all the chasing. It came to a point that I chased him that much that he just gave in. I couldn't believe what I was hearing and the lies that this man was saying. To a massive point, though, deep down it did not surprise me one bit. I knew what he was capable of and knew that he would do or say anything to get him off any charges.

The family trial lasted for around two weeks and quite a few witnesses before it finished and then the waiting game started, wondering and also worrying about what the judge will have to say on her findings and how she would find my parents. That waiting period felt as if it wasn't going to ever end and all kinds of things were going on inside my head, all kinds of scenarios were flying around in my thoughts. The worst outcome, obviously, would be that the judge would favour with my parents and think that they were not guilty of anything and if this was the case, then what outcome would that opinion have on the criminal court hearing that was to follow in the following February? Another scenario that I thought of was that my father would be found not guilty of any findings and be allowed to be released from prison on a tag-like basis until the criminal hearing would occur. I was just terrified that he would be let go or he had found some kind of loophole. When I think the worst I really go deep and I just cannot help but going to that place.

Finally, I received the phone call that I had been waiting for. It was late afternoon, early evening, and my solicitor was there on the phone. I was trying to make out what had happened through listening to the tone of her voice, but she was giving nothing away until she came to the part of the judge's findings. I think I had everything crossed and I was holding my breath and then she told me. Everything in my body just dropped. I released my breath and my shoulders just relaxed and I started to cry. The judge had found them both guilty of all findings. I couldn't believe it. I was in total shock because I strongly believed that somehow, as always, especially my father would have found a way to get out of the trouble he was in as he always did. What was more important to me more than anything, though, was that my words had been listened to and been believed with the help from evidence as well as the witnesses that had defended me. Plus, it was such a good outcome with regard to the criminal hearing that was around the corner.

I couldn't hold it in and I ran down the stairs and told my husband the news and he just got up from his chair, walked over to me and wrapped his arms around me and just held me. No words were spoken or even needed. He just held me whilst I just let the tears flow; it was like the dam was being released of all its water. For the first time in a while I felt a little lighter. I was ready to get myself prepared now for the big one. I could use this experience I had been through to get myself prepared for what was yet to come and I also had to realise that it will be even tougher and the questions were going to be even more difficult as it will be a different process altogether. I could take some hope with me, though, because I had got through it and survived; it was going to make me stronger.

The judge's findings...

I have considered carefully the argument that if what the victim said is true, she would NOT have entered into a consensual relationship with her stepfather which endured for six years, some periods of which were happy, following her reaching 16. It seems necessary, in considering this argument, for me to take into consideration the whole history. The victim was an isolated and abused child in what was, self-evidently, a dysfunctional family even before her sexual relationship with the stepfather. Whilst she ultimately viewed the sexual relationship which commenced in the way (as I am going to find) she alleges as a route to affection which she had not previously, it seems to me that her acceding to and participating in that relationship was more an act of collaboration with her abuser than one of participation in a relationship of equals. That relationship brought her benefits which she had never had before during her childhood, namely affection and esteem.

I have also considered carefully the argument: if what the victim has to say was true, she would never have left her children behind in the care of the stepfather. In deciding this argument, it seems to me I have to take into account that the first time she left, she tried and failed to leave with them. She failed because he found them. That failure has to be set in the context of all of the failed rescues throughout her life, through which I have been going in the chronology. She had fond recollections of the foster home, but ultimately in 1986 when she was just a little girl, nobody had been able to take her away from the misery of the life she was leading at home. Throughout those years there were numerous referrals to Social Services, to the NSPCC, by neighbors, by school staff. None of those interventions were successful in rescuing her from the miserable life that was being led at home. Equally, I have to take into consideration that her own mother had failed to rescue her. This is setting on one side for a moment the issue of failure to protect from sexual abuse; there is an accepted and established failure to protect from physical abuse. The stepfather exercised a terrifying control which no-one, at the time of the victim's departure from the household in 2004, had managed to go beyond in protecting the children of the family. I do consider that it was a huge mistake as to the regard to the victim's younger children, as she indeed herself does, for her to leave those children behind. However, I also consider it likely that she thought that they would be okay, having regard for what she had observed, and that this was her only chance of a proper life of her own and her only chance to escape.

I turn therefore to the findings. I will produce a schedule of the findings I make separate from the reasons.

I do find that the stepfather forced the victim to attempt sexual intercourse with him on several occasions from her being fourteen, dating from the school summer holidays of 1996. He partially penetrated her with his penis on at least two occasions and fully penetrated her in or about November 1996, only shortly after her fifteenth birthday. After that, he forced her to have sexual intercourse with him regularly.

My main reasons for these findings are these:

I am satisfied that the victim is telling the truth about when the stepfather focused predatory sexual attention upon her. She is corroborated in her chronology by other evidence.

I am satisfied from the chronology that she was told she was not his natural daughter in accordance with her account and that of her mother. That telling of her that she was not his natural daughter coincides with her becoming sexually attractive to him as she reached and passed puberty.

I am satisfied, from the general practitioner's records, of when she went on the contraceptive pill (I am going to come back to this when dealing with the mother's role in a moment). That visit to the general practitioner could only have been for the propose of having sex with the stepfather. There is no evidence of her having had other boyfriends; no witness could relate to her having other boyfriends. The only suggestion of other boyfriends is the stepfather's suggestion that in December, when he says he had sex with her for the first time (an account I reject), she was not a virgin. Well, she was not a virgin in December 1997 – that is because he had already had sex with her. There is no evidence of other boyfriends, and so the only purpose of her going on the contraceptive pill at the age of fifteen was to have sex with him. The stepfather's evidence on age overall and his accounts of those first experiences of sexual intercourse overall, for reasons I have outlined when dealing with his evidence, is not credible.

I do find that the stepfather forced the victim to have oral sex with him on multiple occasions from her being fifteen. There has not been a deal of the oral evidence in relation to this matter, but overall, where there is conflict between the victim and the stepfather, I accept her account by reason of my overall assessment of her credibility contrasted with his.

Findings against the mother.

The mother knew about the sexual abuse of the victim by the stepfather and did nothing to protect her.

The mother, on occasions, brought the victim into hers and the father's bedroom, knowing that he would force her to engage in sexual acts, including intercourse, while she was there.

On one occasion on holiday in Menorca, the father alternated between attempting to penetrate the victim's vagina with his erect penis and having sexual intercourse with the mother; all three were in the same room.

The mother took the victim to the GP for her to be prescribed contraception when she was just fifteen years of age, when she knew, or ought to have known, that the contraception was to protect the victim from becoming pregnant by the stepfather, whom she knew, or ought to have known, was either having, or was intent on having, sexual intercourse with her.

My reasons for the findings against the mother.

I make these findings against the mother with a heavy heart. Unlike the allegations against the stepfather, where I am satisfied that what I have found is true to a criminal standard, in this instance my findings are based on a conclusion that what the victim says about this is more likely to be true than what the mother is saying. I am not saying this on a fine balance; I am very clearly satisfied to the civil standard. The evidence drives me to these conclusions despite my own reluctance, in common, I suspect, with almost all the people listening to this evidence, to accept it could be true. I quite accept that the mother's actions and inactions were brought about by her terror of that of the partner and her inability to escape him over many years. His domination of her was terrifying and absolute and she was as much a victim as the daughter.

I am persuaded in coming to these conclusions by the victim's demeanor in describing this part of the evidence. Her vacillation between genuine sympathy for her mother, whom she had seen abused and victimized over the years and a heartfelt bewilderment and hurt at her mother's failure to protect her was extremely persuasive.

I rely, in making these findings, on the mother's paucity as a witness by way of her changing accounts. Her answers to me in the middle of her evidence when she was describing how giving evidence was so painful, that it was like looking through a window at events that were happening, and she simply could not see a failure to protect from sexual abuse, or the sexual abuse at all that was alleged. I asked her, as I was reminded by her team's submissions, whether she thought she would be able to say so, even if she did see that and she told me that she did not know. It is actually my conclusion that she would not, at the moment, have the capacity to say so, even if it was true.

My impression, as I have also described, is that her victimhood has stripped her of the capacity for empathy for others. The earlier failures to act to protect from physical abuse are very serious and it seems to me, a harbinger of those failures to protect the victim from sexual abuse. This woman's emotional survival has depended on her closing her eyes and not questioning her partner.

It seems to me, finally, that the mother's passivity remaining in the household where her daughter had supplanted her role as partner following the information of the so-called relationship for a period of, what I think was some three or four years hints at the passivity that would be required for the failures to protect the victim and is an echo of it. It is an extraordinary piece of the narrative that this very strange family remained together so long after the victim's so-called relationship with the stepfather emerged, particularly so far as the mother is concerned.

Other Findings to be Taken into Account.

The stepfather was violent to the victim during the relationship. On two occasions he punched the victim to the mouth. On one of those occasions he knocked part of her tooth out; he also threatened her with a gun.

I have explained this finding in relating my views as to the credibility of the stepfather and the victim. Also, these allegations are consistent with all the others that are made and my assessment of the credibility of other witness.

The mother knew about and failed to protect the victim from the physical abuse perpetrated by the stepfather. In relation to that finding, it seems to me impossible to make the findings that are conceded by the stepfather.

Chapter 13

I was so relieved to get that trial over with; in a way I could see it as a practice run for the bigger case. This drained me in a big way, both physically and emotionally. It brought on more seizures; I was having up to sixty a week. I couldn't go out on my own, and still I can't. The reason being when I have a seizure now and, say, I bang my head or my head takes most of the impact, it causes me to have a memory lapse and I lose my current memory. Not only that, but the other injuries that I suffered throughout the seizures. I practically lived in my bedroom in the month leading up to the criminal case. I couldn't face anything; days rolled into days and I didn't care about myself, to be honest. Then I received a phone call from the leading officer of my case and I had to go back to my home town to the courts to meet with the CPS and if I wanted to, to have a look around the courts to see where I was to give my evidence and the courtroom in which the hearing would take place. To this, when it was put to me, I declined. It was getting to the point where I was getting sick and tired of seeing a courtroom and couldn't wait to see the back of them.

Here we were in February 2016 and the start of the court case. I remember the journey on that early morning train, bobbing along the rail tracks, and all I could feel was dread and anxiety building up in the pit of my stomach. The closer I got, the bigger and tighter that knot was getting; fear was building as I wondered what the defense for my parents were going to throw at me. Also, I was second guessing myself all the time, but knowing that this was it; no turning around now. I had a big job on my hands to make twelve strangers not only listen to me and what I had to say, but I had to make them believe me. To be honest, this was the bit that terrified me, as for the jury hearing all this, what would they think? Some of them may never have come across anything like this in their lives. Some may have heard of it in the past through other cases or heard something on the news, but to be part of a jury in a case such as this, what would they really think? Could or would they believe that such things do happen? I was truly putting my faith in twelve strangers, hoping and praying that they would know that I was telling the truth.

The first day of the trial was very long and with a lot of waiting around whilst things were being sorted out and evidence being talked about, what all parties wanted to use and what not to use. Finally, after waiting around for around three hours it was time for me to go into the private room where I was to give my evidence via video link. Even though I was not in the courtroom, I was still in the same building this time and I was in so much fear. I was so terrified that I was cutting my arms quite badly with my nails. I was using my nails to go over the same mark over and over again until the blood was seeping out. I think the lady that was with me was concerned and I think she may have mentioned something to the officer and to the CPS. The reason why I think this is because after I had spent that first afternoon giving evidence, they were there waiting for me when I came out the room wanting to talk to me. Giving me advice and letting me know that it was important I was in the right head space; otherwise the hearing couldn't go ahead. I explained that I didn't want that to happen, so I walked back to the train station worried about how I could overcome the fear because the last thing I wanted was for the court case to fall through.

The officer in charge of the case was already on it, though, without me knowing. He had got straight onto the phone to my husband and explained what had happened in court and how they were worried about me. They offered to pay for his train fare to be with me the next two to three days and my husband managed to get a close friend to babysit our two younger children. Things were put into place to help me and to support me. I was so grateful I couldn't tell you; knowing that I was not going to be there on my own made all the difference. After that I was as strong as I could possibly be and I didn't back down. I think, at times, I was a bit forceful as I thought that the defense weren't listening to me at times or would interrupt me. I can actually remember telling, I think it was my mother's lawyer, "Excuse me, but can you wait until I have finished what I was saying." I don't know what happened to me at times. It was as if an inner voice was roaring and I was going to be listened to. When I needed a break because quite a few times the questioning got very heavy and I needed to compose myself the judge allowed it. My husband was there and he would talk about anything and everything, never about the case. He would always want to take my mind away from it and try to put a smile on my face or try to make me laugh, to which, to be fair, he has always been good at doing.

Then finally after three, three and a half days it was over. I had done all that I could; my part was finished with. It was time for the other witnesses who had witnessed things I had gone through to give their evidence; then it would be my

159

parents' turn to take the stand. First, it would be my mother, then it would be the turn of my father. I had the option to go and listen to them give their defense, but do you know what? I didn't want to go. I didn't want to sit there and listen to their lies. I didn't want them to have the satisfaction to see me hurt or cry. I was done with them; they were getting no more of me.

Then finally, after two- and a-bit weeks, the hearing was over with and the jury was allowed to leave the courtroom to go into their own private room to discuss what they thought was the verdict. We needed the jury to be unanimous in their verdict, as the CPS didn't want a majority. The jury took two hours to reach a decision for both my parents. So here I was again, fretting at home waiting for the police officer to ring me with that verdict. Questions flying through my head: had I done enough? Would it have had more of an impact if I gave my evidence there on the stand in front of them? How many would have fallen for my father's charm? For those few hours it was as though time had stood still and the hand of the clock was just ticking louder and louder. Then suddenly, the phone started to ring and I recall reaching out to take the phone and my hand was shaking so badly and my armpits started to sweat really badly. A small part of me wanted to ignore the phone; I didn't want to know in case it was bad news. I answered the phone and it was the leading police officer. He explained that the papers had been there and had wanted to talk to me as they were writing the story and it was to be put in the local newspaper. Then the moment came to discussing the verdict. My father got found guilty of all charges and my mother got found guilty of ill-treatment. My stepfather was jailed for twenty-five years and my mother received an eighteen-month sentence.

I was so overwhelmed and happy with the outcome and relieved for it to be finally over. I spoke to the papers and they put it to press. I was wondering if I did the right thing in speaking to the papers or should I have let them write the story just from the information they had? Now, though, I am glad I spoke to them because at the end of the day they were going to print the story regardless. At least if I spoke to them, they would get key points right. There was another side to it as well, and that is the reason for writing this book, for my voice to be heard and to get my story out there, because if it helps others and helps them to come forward, then I have done something worthwhile.

Chapter 14

Four years have passed now and I am in a far happier place. It has taken a lot to get to where I am, with a lot of help and support. Yes, I am still under the Mental Health Services – some medications have now changed and I am awaiting to receive Psychotherapy. So I have come on hugely in regard to my mental health. Would I have wanted to receive psychotherapy a couple of years ago, then the answer would have been 'hell no' as I wasn't ready.

Do I have any regrets in regard to going to the police and reporting my parents' crimes? That is a really good question, especially looking back on it now. However, if truth be told, then no I do not have any regrets whatsoever. As much as it was extremely difficult at the time and a lot of other issues regarding other people, I am glad I did what I did and I feel better and stronger as a woman to be able to say that I finally stood up and faced my abusers. At long last I feel free from the hold that they had over me for so long.

Things are starting to be normal again. However, don't get me wrong, I have a lot more good days now, but, I can still have the odd bad day here and there. It's how I deal with the bad days that builds me up, putting everything into practise what I have learnt along the way. I hope that my words will at least help ones out there in the world to reach out and come forward, I hope that my experiences bring hope to those, that no matter what, no matter how long time has gone by you will be listened to. Don't suffer in silence like I did, because in the end it is you that suffers the most. Deal with things as soon as you can because running away from it, does a lot more damage to you, in time, mentally and physically. If this even helps that one person than it has all be worthwhile.

CPSIA information can be obtained
at www.ICGtesting.com
Printed in the USA
LVHW111639170422
716440LV00006B/643

9 781788 308267